"By challenging us to look at leadership in an unfamiliar frame, the i4 model offers new insights into ourselves and others - insights that are founded in the science of our brains and behaviours - that will ultimately enable us to be better leaders who can adapt and thrive in a complex, ever evolving, global business landscape."

Dr. Lana Ledgerwood
Cognitive Neuroscientist & Leadership Consultant, Heidrick & Struggles

~

"Leadership is not improvised. Leadership is learnt and developed. In her new book, Silvia Damiano gives us the key: the i4 model. In a world characterised by complexity, uncertainty and globalisation, the four skills Damiano includes in her Model (integration, inspiration, imagination and intuition) are essential for individual and group success."

Dr. Nestor Braidot
Author of NeuroManagement & CEO of Braidot Group (Business & Neuroscience)

~

"My brain so enjoyed Silvia's deliciously structured description on how my neurobiology and neurochemistry can alter so that I can start exhibiting some of the leadership behaviours I have been trying to exhibit at work but somehow have failed. My brain really does want to know the chemicals, wiring and restructuring it needs to achieve in order to change behaviour on the outside. Silvia has done a wonderful job at giving my brain the manual on how to achieve that end state. The brains of leaders will enjoy Silvia's work immensely."

Katharine McLennan
Head of Global Leadership Academy, QBE

~

"Intrepid. Intriguing. Insightful. Invigorating. Silvia Damiano takes you to a place that compels you to challenge what you know – or think you know – about leadership. A fantastic read where its true beauty is in the simplicity of its deconstruction and re-construction of notions and principles. I found myself constantly questioning my actions and inactions as a leader and gained far greater insight of my influence towards others – positive and negative – regardless of my intent."

Milano Pellegrini
HR Executive, Consultant & Lecturer

LEADERSHIP IS UPSIDE DOWN

THE i4 NEUROLEADER REVOLUTION

~

Silvia Damiano

with
Juan Carlos Cubeiro & Tao de Haas

~

In memory of Nelson Mandela (1918–2013).
One of the greatest leaders of all times,
who died at age 95 during the writing of this book.

~

ABOUT THE AUTHOR

SILVIA DAMIANO

Silvia Damiano is the CEO of the About my Brain Institute, Adjunct Director of Neuro-Learning programs at Macquarie Graduate School of Management (MGSM) in Sydney and the Founder of the BrainArt Project.

Silvia is originally from Buenos Aires, Argentina and has studied Biological Sciences, Sociology and Neuroscience of Leadership. Silvia has worked in Latin America, South Africa, Europe and Australia, where she currently lives.

An award-winning educator, a researcher and a creative entrepreneur, Silvia has worked for companies such as Telecom in Argentina, Ernst & Young in Chile and Westpac Bank in Australia. She consults, trains and coaches individuals and teams to improve leadership and business performance.

Silvia is a highly experienced master facilitator, an inspiring speaker and the author of the best-selling book "Engage Me" and many articles on staff engagement, emotional intelligence and neuroleadership.

Website:
www.aboutmybrain.com/silviadamiano

Twitter:
@silviadamiano

Facebook:
www.facebook.com/silviadamiano

LinkedIn:
www.linkedin.com/in/silviadamiano

Google Plus:
www.google.com/+SilviaDamiano

ABOUT THE CONTRIBUTORS

JUAN CARLOS CUBEIRO

Juan Carlos Cubeiro is the Head of Talent at Manpower Group & CEO of Right Management in Spain. He is also the Honorary President of the Spanish Executive Coaching Association (AECOP). Juan Carlos was born in Madrid and after studying Economics, Law and International Marketing, he worked for Arthur Andersen, Coopers & Lybrand (now PwC) and the HayGroup.

With more than 25 years of experience in Strategic Consulting, Leadership and Coaching, Juan Carlos is the author of more than 40 books, including "A Sense of Flow", "Guardiola Leadership" and "Why You Need A Coach". An international speaker, from Shanghai to Chicago, from London to Santiago de Chile, he is considered one of the top strategic coaches worldwide and has recently been awarded the 2014 Humanistic Leader Prize in Spain.

TAO DE HAAS

Tao de Haas is a Psychotherapist, Executive Coach and Corporate Educator, who specialises in management and leadership development.

Tao was born in Utrecht in the Netherlands. He is a registered psychotherapist and a clinical member of the Psychotherapist and Counselling Federation of Australia. Tao has a Master's degree in Applied Science (Social Ecology). Tao is a published author and makes regular appearances on national radio and television.

ACKNOWLEDGEMENTS

Life is easier when we collaborate with others towards a common goal. This book is written with the help of selfless individuals whom I have had the pleasure of meeting and befriending.

Without these individuals, achieving the daunting task of writing a book would not be possible. To all of you: my fabulous personal editors Elleanor Kearsley (in Tasmania), Melissa Dumas (in Sydney), Pandora Varley (in Melbourne) and Twin Miracles Editorial (in Houston, US), my translator Paulina Freire (in Quito, Ecuador), and my incredible designers Relmi Damiano and Su Jung Kim, I extend my most sincere appreciation.

You made this book a reality and I will be forever grateful.

To my collaborators Juan Carlos Cubeiro (in Madrid) and Tao de Haas (in Sydney) who willingly took up the challenge of listening to my ideas, reviewing and analysing the content and spreading the word in regards to the i4 Model - how gracious and professional you have been by sharing your expertise, knowledge and perspectives.

And to the many others who have helped me consolidate my thoughts; to everyone who attended the first i4 Practitioner Certification Program in Sydney; to all those around the world who were the subjects of my interviews and investigations; and to the participants in my workshops and coaching sessions - your wisdom and insights have been a critical contribution towards feeding my brain to develop this new framework. This work, I hope, will last eternally and I could not have done it without the support I have received from each of you.

I would also like to extend a very special thanks to my parents, for always being there for me, no matter what happens; to my partner Carl for putting up with endless weekends of writing, traveling and working and to Robin Wigsten for his ongoing support of Relmi during this time and also for his strategic insights.

Finally, I would like to dedicate this book to my children. You are living proof that believing in people and helping them grow is both a plausible and rewarding strategy. You are my inspiration, as you represent all the children that are yet to enter this world, who could benefit from workplaces that treat people respectfully, and who deserve to live in a society that is more balanced.

Silvia Damiano
Founder & CEO
About my Brain Institute

THIS WORK, I HOPE, WILL LAST ETERNALLY
AND I COULD NOT HAVE DONE IT WITHOUT
THE SUPPORT I HAVE RECEIVED FROM
EACH OF YOU.

FOREWORD
BY JOANNE KEEN

There are certain people who enter your life who are life changing. Leadership expert Silvia Damiano is one such person.

Through her incredible insight, knowledge, intuition and innate ability to engage with people from many varied backgrounds, Silvia inspires others to not only strive to be better than their best but become the type of leader who others want to follow.

In "Leadership is Upside Down", Silvia provides invaluable concepts to enable anyone and everyone to unlock their potential and create their own personal leadership style. This ensures that regardless of our position or title, we are able to inspire, motivate and empower others to excel and create a more positive, engaged and productive culture to meet the demands of the new 'era of work'.

This is particularly critical in today's world, as according to Silvia's research, people are now, more than ever, looking to their leaders, co-workers and organisations' values and culture to inspire them and create an environment in which they can excel.

This was something that was previously unheard of; probably since without technology constantly linking us back to the workplace and blurring the lines between our home and work lives, it was far easier to disconnect from the office once we returned home at the end of the day.

The increasing demands of the modern workplace makes it essential to our own success and the success of our co-workers and organisations, that we have the necessary skills and understanding to ensure that we get the very best not only from ourselves but also from others.

Historically, it seems that in many organisations, people felt that the responsibility for creating a positive and collaborative culture lay solely with the leaders at the top of the organisation and that there was little (if any) contribution that could be made by those within the lower ranks.

Silvia proposes to look at leadership through a new lens; turning the pyramid upside down and encouraging us all, regardless of where we sit in our organisational structure, to start exploring the special powers that live within us to become more confident, energetic, conscientious and generous.

What this means is that it is no longer necessary for us to wait until we are promoted or receive a leadership title to start making a positive impact on our own lives and the lives of others - we all have the ability to provide influence and make a real and positive difference.

This is not only exciting, but empowering to us all; as it means that leadership is no longer simply about a title and hierarchical structure, but rather an ability to collaborate, work together and create a more engaged, motivated and productive workforce - attributes which are essential in today's economy.

The i4 Neuroleader Model is an invaluable concept to anyone who wants to develop as an exceptional leader. By providing a greater insight and understanding firstly of ourselves and then of others, the i4 Neuroleader Model empowers us to make a real and positive impact upon our professional and personal lives and those of others and ensures that we have the skills and knowledge to be a catalyst for change.

The model has been created as a result of many years of Silvia's work in the field of leadership development and is reflective of the interactions that she has had with a diverse range of people from various backgrounds and positions, who have an inherent desire to become inspirational and transformational leaders.

The exciting thing about the i4 Neuroleader Model is that the key abilities (integration, inspiration, imagination, intuition) exist inside all of us. If properly cultivated, nurtured and developed, they will ensure not only that we reach our greatest potential, but also ensure that our co-workers, organisations and communities do the same.

How revolutionary!

Joanne Keen
General Counsel
Energex Limited

THIS BOOK HAS BEEN WRITTEN TO
ENCOURAGE NEW PERSPECTIVES ON
HOW TO VIEW PEOPLE'S CAPABILITIES
IN THE 21ST CENTURY.

THIS BOOK IS A CO-CREATION.
IT IS NOT ACADEMIC BUT RATHER
CONCEPTUAL AND PRACTICAL.

THIS BOOK HAS NO FORMAL
INTRODUCTION, INSTEAD IT BEGINS
WITH A POEM. ➔

I dream of a time...
When people who have the power, learn to show humility.
When those who become obsessed with getting everything right,
come to understand that on occasion,
it is absolutely fine to get it wrong.

I dream of a time...
When the analytical learn that communicating with others,
can make all the difference.
And when those who are aggressive,
learn to manage their impulses and be kind to others.

When those who have great vision,
become comfortable with looking at the smaller details.
And when those who lack patience,
realise that their impatience makes others anxious.

I dream of a time...
When those who are financially successful,
learn that helping others in need, is good for the soul.
When those who yell,
realise that intimidation is disengaging.

When those who show indecision,
learn that they are creating doubt in their followers.
And when those who are controlling,
learn that empowering others is more rewarding.

I dream of a time...
When those who do not want to change,
learn that they are missing out on the mystery of the unknown
and when those who wish to be the centre of attention,
learn that they are not the priority of others.

When people realise that leaders who care, are the better leaders.
And when people understand that developing our own leadership
is essential for a better humanity.

~

Silvia Damiano

CONTENTS →

Section One

ON LEADERSHIP &
THE i4 MODEL

~

This section approaches the topic of leadership from a story telling perspective.

It also explores the rationale and ideology that underpin the creation of the i4 NeuroLeader Model.

~

Chapter One

LEADERSHIP IS UPSIDE DOWN

CREATING THE LEADER IN YOU

This is a book focused on leadership; personal leadership. It is not about discussing the styles of the greatest leaders in history or complex academic theories that few can relate to; it is about your own individual, unique leadership.

The type of leadership you may want to work on so you can improve what you do each day. Or perhaps the type you wish to develop in order to become a more inspiring person to those who you come in contact with, throughout your life and working career.

Or maybe you possess the type of leadership that you could easily enhance by tapping into your existing strengths? I am sure you may have heard this idea about using your strengths rather than trying to improve your weaknesses, but consider this - what if we didn't have to constantly and endlessly compare our strengths to those of others, trying to emulate them to become a better person or leader?

To reiterate: this book is about you. The thoughts in this text are dedicated to helping, guiding and offering different perspectives on how you can create the leader in you.

HOW IT ALL STARTED

In August 2011, while flying over the Australian Red Centre from Perth to Sydney, I had a sudden insight and asked myself:

Isn't it time to update leadership models? What if a model could better reflect current business requirements? Wouldn't it be great if different segments of the working population were included in some way?

I never imagined that I would be conceptualising a leadership model, let alone writing a book about it! But then I thought, "Why not? If I can think about it, why not put pen to paper and do it?"

Each day, I meet more and more people interested in learning how to develop their leadership capabilities. There is definitely a big appetite for it and obviously I am not the only one that thinks along these lines.

When I came across leadership guru Gary Hamel's latest challenge – I felt joy in my heart. His initiative, entitled "Leaders Everywhere", responds to the thought that ⊕

"We live in a world where leadership has never before been so necessary, but where leaders so often seem to come up short."

If we think of past models and frameworks, the reality is that they fit nicely within predominantly male-dominated and 'homogeneous' work environments, where command, control and certain types of leadership traits worked reasonably well.

Things have changed dramatically in the last 20 years, and what people expect from their leaders and organisations today is completely different to what they expected many years ago.

In my case, I represent the female gender, working mothers and someone who has worked with different generations. I would like to think that I can put myself in the shoes of a few groups.

After many years of recommending a wide variety of well-known models and regurgitating famous experts' lists of leadership attributes, I have come to believe that a need has arisen when it comes to describing how a leader may look in today's world, a need that I am endeavouring to fill.

What I am talking about are 'models' that can potentially bring a more balanced approach to how both genders and different generations view and interpret leadership; and that can also highlight how brain function influences a leader's performance.

The response to these thoughts was the creation of the i4 Neuroleader Model (in short – the i4 Model), which I feel very excited to introduce to you in this book.

Leadership models, frameworks and principles have always been useful in helping people to understand where leaders need to focus their efforts. They can also assist in pinpointing specific skills or behaviours that seem important to people or organisations at a particular moment in time.

A great example of this would be the popular book "7 Habits of Highly Effective People", which outlined a set of principles that launched American author Stephen Covey into fame.

The way we work has shifted since 1989, the year when Covey's book was first published. And even though some principles never die, the work environment has become more complex than we could have ever imagined.

As an example, employees now look forward to being inspired by their bosses and their organisations' values and methods. This was something that was previously unheard of; perhaps because once an employee left the office, there was no digital device in their hands to keep them thinking about work.

Then, there is the case of those who enjoy not being called 'employees' or having a boss at all. They are more commonly referred to as associates, freelancers or contractors, and they would rather move without restraint from project to project and from organisation to organisation.

All this has prompted me to think about an array of possible scenarios ⊙➔

WHAT IF, AS A RESULT OF AN ESCALATING DEMAND FOR 'MORE AND BETTER', SENIOR MANAGEMENT SIMPLY COULD NOT COPE WITH LEADING OTHERS?

WHAT IF EVERYONE NEEDED TO MAKE SOME KIND OF BEHAVIOURAL CONTRIBUTION TO SOLVE THIS LEADERSHIP DILEMMA?

WHAT IF THERE WAS NO PLACE TO HIDE OR DISGUISE REDUCED PRODUCTIVITY, IN EXCHANGE FOR A MONTHLY CHEQUE?

WHAT IF THE BIASED MANAGER WHO HAS 'FAVOURITES' WAS NO LONGER IN A POSITION TO PROTECT THEM WHEN IT COMES TO POOR PERFORMANCE?

WHAT IF THE WORLD OF BUSINESS
ENDS UP WITH FLATTER ORGANISATIONS
WHERE 'THE BOSS' IS NO LONGER NEEDED?

In fact, this is already happening.

I could go on and list pages of rhetorical questions when it comes to the future of leadership, but that would just feed the problem and defeat the purpose.

While some of us are willing to think about the leadership topic, I find that too few are really willing to try new solutions in order to resolve the issues that have arisen with the progression of modern society.

In a recent study by the University of Sydney and Australian BOSS magazine, it emerged that 25% of a group of business executives think their companies are being 'over-managed' and 'under-led'; and remarkably, just 5% think that developing good leaders is something their companies take seriously.

It appears that the main focus continues to be on 'management' and how efficiently people are able to drive profit or run a business, rather than on leadership. The conclusion stemming from this research is that more time and recognition should be dedicated to developing leaders.

While there are many definitions of leadership, one I like is by Kevin Kruse. In his article for Forbes Magazine he defines leadership as ⊕

"A process of social influence, which maximises the efforts of others towards the achievement of a goal".

In my opinion, leadership starts from within. The better we learn to lead ourselves, the better we will be at leading others. In turn, this will encourage superior performance levels, which may translate into improved decision-making, better-thought strategies and higher quality interactions with others.

But all is not lost. Some companies such as Michigan's Menlo Innovations are already being led to work along these lines. Menlo is a consulting and software development company in the United States.

Menlo's fruitful implementations include: people pairing to do work, with no one working alone; workspaces that are open and collaborative; mindsets that promote making mistakes faster to enhance learning; pet and baby friendly offices and constant learning and mentoring, just to name a few.

On Menlo's website (www.menloinnovations.com), founders Richard Goebel and James Sheridan openly share the secret of their culture by stating that it all comes down to leadership.

THE BEST TYPE OF LEADERSHIP IS THAT WHICH HELPS THOSE AROUND
YOU PRODUCE BETTER RESULTS THAN THEY WOULD ON THEIR OWN.
IT'S NOT ABOUT HIERARCHY OR AUTHORITY.

WE WANT TO DEVELOP LEADERS WITHIN MENLO WHO THINK
ABOUT HOW TO LEVERAGE THEIR SKILLS AND EXPERIENCES
TO SUPPORT THOSE AROUND THEM.

WE ACKNOWLEDGE THAT WE ALL HAVE ROOM TO GROW IN THIS AREA,
BUT ARE COMMITTED TO CONTINUOUS IMPROVEMENT.
THIS IS WHAT TEAM, INNOVATION AND COLLABORATION IS ALL ABOUT.

Richard Goebel and James Sheridan

With such an inspiring real-life example, the question I pose here is ➡

WHAT NEEDS TO HAPPEN FOR PEOPLE TO REALISE THAT TAKING THE TIME TO 'REFLECT' IS THE STARTING POINT FOR GROWTH AND CHANGE?

DISRUPTING LEADERSHIP

People are so absorbed with the vast distractions of the digital world and obsessed with the financials that the inclination for working on 'oneself' and learning to empathise with others has disappeared off the radar.

Having reflected on my life so far, past management experiences and what I teach others in the leadership domain, I find that it is vital to continually remind myself to keep discovering and learning ways of looking at what I do and how I do it.

I also recognise the importance of working through my limitations (i.e. learning to accept and use new technologies faster). Although I don't necessarily succeed all the time when it comes to the latest advancements, I humbly accept that in certain aspects of the business, I am better off working with younger minds that are, without a doubt, more knowledgeable than me in these matters.

I can certainly say that this definitely was not the mindset I had earlier in my career, when age defined a certain level of wisdom and respect for my elders meant they were usually 'always right'.

With society and technology changing faster than ever, wisdom and even patience are no longer considered blissful qualities as they used to be. Developing leadership consists of unlearning and relearning. It is crucial to make an effort to ensure that any existing 'cob webs' in our brains do not become worthless beliefs which can hold us back when it comes to adapting to the current times.

It is this need to clear out old ways of thinking which brings to my mind a quote from Luke Williams, author of the book, "Disrupt" ➔

"

THE INTERNET AND THE INFRASTRUCTURE OF MASSIVE CONNECTION HAS REINVENTED MANY INDUSTRIES... BUT WE ARE STILL SURROUNDED BY COUNTLESS PRODUCTS, SERVICES AND BUSINESS MODELS BUILT ON THE LOGIC OF THE PAST.

MANY OF THE DECISIONS THAT DEFINE THESE BUSINESSES WERE MADE YEARS AGO, IN A DIFFERENT AGE, AND IN A DIFFERENT CONTEXT.

WE NEED TO RETHINK THE HABITS THAT HAVE MADE US SUCCESSFUL IN THE PAST AND CHALLENGE THE CONVENTIONAL WISDOM AND INDUSTRY MODELS THAT HAVE DEFINED OUR WORLD.

Luke Williams

THE TIME HAS COME TO REASSESS LEADERSHIP

Collectively, once we start re-thinking our habits, we will discover that some of the mindsets and behaviours that have served us in the past may no longer be helpful.

The need to make some changes, as uncomfortable as this may sound, is the best way forward if we are to adapt to this new ever-changing reality.

Over the past fifteen years, little advancement has been made in reshaping traditional leadership models; however, in the field of neuroscience, new insights into how our brains work offer the opportunity to better understand why and how people behave, make decisions and engage with others.

It seems natural to include the brain in a leadership model.

After all, this incredible organ is home to our intellect, memories, emotions, discernment and much more. But the brain is **not** the only organ in our body that matters. There are other bodily processes that have been relegated and in many cases forgotten, when it comes to leadership and management practices.

From my perspective, these 'body processes' can be expressed with the following terms and descriptions:

○ **Integration**
   The ability to unify brain, mind and body.

○ **Inspiration**
   The ability to manage our energy and stimulate our minds

○ **Imagination**
   The mental ability which facilitates creative thinking

○ **Intuition**
   The ability to understand something instinctively

IT IS TIME TO REKINDLE, UTILISE AND NURTURE THESE ABILITIES TO HELP LEADERS IMPROVE THEIR EFFECTIVENESS IN NEW WAYS.

THE ADVENTURE STARTS

In 2010, I set myself the goal of interviewing at least 250 women and men from around the world with varied backgrounds and levels of experience. They included CEOs, executives, managers and entrepreneurs, who led teams both large and small.

I also found it important to interview individuals who were not in 'formal' leadership positions, but who had to deal with people as part of their roles on a frequent basis.

This research provided me with extraordinary insights. When I combined this data with all the experiences from leadership workshops and coaching sessions, I realised that these encounters were allowing me to delve deeper into people's minds and better understand their concerns about how to lead successfully in today's world.

All of these interviews, alongside other carefully planned surveys and discussions with colleagues, led me to some very interesting discoveries.

For example, when it comes to leadership development, the majority of people who work for organisations, although having participated in some kind of leadership development program throughout their careers, could not recall the nuances or details of intricate leadership models.

For those of us who work in the fields of Human Resources and Organisational Development, this finding can be rather disappointing, yet quite understandable.

Much like a designer preaching about the importance of typography to a fitness instructor, the importance will never be conveyed between the two.

However, this is not to say that when individuals have the time to read books on leadership or are exposed to powerful concepts such as the Johari window – a framework that helps people understand the importance of feedback to discover their blind spots – that they are not going to show interest or be inclined to learn more about the subject.

LEADERSHIP MODELS

In my experience, even if the details or the names of leadership models and frameworks are forgotten, the things that seem to mostly stick in people's brains are:

- The effectiveness of the presenters.

- The sense of enjoyment that comes with the opportunity to listen to new or relevant content within the context of their reality at work.

- The powerful effect of assessment results (especially those that are unexpected).

- The interactions with peers who share similar issues.

- The positive emotions associated with self-derived solutions which emerge when participants are fully immersed in a face-to-face, high quality leadership program.

It is the memories and emotions felt in a face to face environment that have a deeper impact with participants in comparison to the virtual experience. This could also be what motivates people to think more seriously about changing what is currently not working for them.

Many people have told me that it was 'that leadership workshop' five years ago that prompted them to start thinking about their own approach; and since that 'aha' moment, they have never returned to doing some of the things that had previously limited their performance. Being able to generate an insight moment is the starting point of any change process. This is powerful.

This feeling is similar to the sensation of going to a concert and experiencing goose bumps when your favourite artist takes the stage. Imagine the emotions you experience when you hear them 'live' versus the ones felt when listening to the same artist at home, alone.

While goose bumps may still arise, the intensity of the emotion and the memories from the event are what our brains recollect. This is what makes it unforgettable and creates the energy necessary to start any kind of change..

FROM TOP TO BOTTOM
OR FROM BOTTOM TO TOP?

For as long as I have been practicing, leadership development has been secretly safeguarded and run mainly at senior and middle management levels, with very few organisations passing these lessons onto lower levels.

There are a number of reasons for this, but the main one would be limited training budgets. The other reason is the mistaken belief that a manager, who has not even unravelled the mysteries of leadership, can effortlessly duplicate these lessons with their teams in addition to his/her daily tasks, usually of a more operational nature.

All too often, the development of top level leaders is hindered due to a lack of time or lack of acceptance about their need for development, especially if they are already successful. Most commonly, it is inflated egos that steer clear from public vulnerability, in particular when feedback or assessments are involved.

With this, many opt for private executive coaching sessions, where their issues are kept isolated from the rest of the team, their identities safeguarded and their leadership weaknesses completely hidden.

Of course, there are stories of great CEOs who accepted the challenge and openly embraced the need to undertake personal changes to help improve the culture of the organisation, and consequently the share price, engagement levels and productivity.

In my view, it is only the minority who appear willing to emulate these more courageous leaders. I am hoping this will start to change. We need our organisations and societies led by 'conscious' rather than 'unconscious' leaders.

CONFESSIONS

I would like to share some of the findings from my interviews which you may identify with. An interesting one was people wanting to 'confess' – as if it was some kind of crime, the 'strong internal need' to become more 'balanced' – so they could better withstand the demands of today's workplaces.

Others mentioned high doses of frustration associated with the inability to fulfil diverse expectations from team members, clients and colleagues; expectations that usually change with gender, age, level of expertise and cultural background, and that at times, can overwhelm them.

As a consequence of this, there was a clear sense of apprehension about feeling limited in their capacity to inspire and influence the people around them. There were a few senior leaders who acknowledged the incessant pressure from the top to move quickly, deal with complex issues and make the 'right' decisions without failing in the attempt.

In many cases, particularly at middle and senior management levels, the pressure to perform and do more each day feels very real to them, to the point of almost feeling disabled and unsuitable if they don't satisfy everyone else's expectations and demands.

THE INCEPTION OF THE i4 NEUROLEADER MODEL

With these revelations, the idea of creating a new model presented itself in my mind with crystal clarity. I imagined a model that could be both simple and easily remembered; and that could suit anyone and everyone, no matter how big or small their business is – independent of seniority, gender, generation or cultural background.

I also had a strong yearning to create a leadership model that would cater for the other half of the world's population – women. I believe women have their own views about what leadership is and how they want to tackle it, despite the obstacles that many still endure in workplaces around the world today.

Having this aspiration motivated me to include words like 'intuition' in the model; a word that in the years to come will no longer be considered taboo in the business world. 'Intuition' is an ability **that is transgender**, even though many people do not wish to use such a term at the business table.

A recent example of how times are changing in relation to how people communicate and talk about intuition is the case of Alexa Von Tobel, founder and CEO of Learnvest.com.

In an interview, Alexa, a Harvard graduate and former Morgan Stanley employee, tells the story of how she started her own business by basically trusting her gut, which made all the difference. She says ➲

I KNEW IN MY GUT IMMEDIATELY THAT THE TIME HAD COME
WHEN PEOPLE REALLY NEEDED FINANCIAL ADVICE.

IN SOME WAY, I INTUITIVELY KNEW THAT ACCESSING FINANCIAL
ADVICE ONLINE COULD BE BOTH AFFORDABLE AND EFFECTIVE
FOR PEOPLE.

ESTABLISHING THE COUNTRY'S FIRST ONLINE FINANCIAL
PLANNING SERVICE WAS THE SCARIEST THING I DID,
BUT IT WAS THE BEST DECISION I HAVE EVER MADE.

Alexa Von Tobel

A MODEL THAT SPEAKS TO EVERYONE

Since its inception, the i4 Model has been socialised with many of my clients and peers who were open and interested to hear my story and rationale.

Needless to say, I was ecstatic when they confirmed that it made perfect sense, particularly because the model allowed them to validate their thoughts in regards to what type of 'competencies' are most required in today's global economy.

These competencies are:

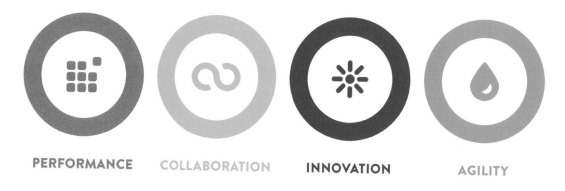

PERFORMANCE   COLLABORATION   INNOVATION   AGILITY

THE i4 MODEL AIMS TO START A DIFFERENT
LEADERSHIP CONVERSATION.

THE POTENTIAL APPLICATIONS FOR
PEOPLE'S PROFESSIONAL AND PERSONAL
LIVES ARE VAST.

Chapter Two

FROM LEADERS TO NEUROLEADERS

I NOT ONLY USE ALL THE BRAINS I HAVE, BUT ALL I CAN BORROW.

Woodrow Wilson, US President, 1914

BRAIN FRENZY

As I walk through the streets of New York, I am engrossed in a crowd of people. All sizes, ages, accents, fashions and nationalities, passing me by like a running stream. My attention is captured as I notice a large number of people consumed by their phones and other devices – either talking, scrolling or tapping away – connecting with thousands of others, doing the same thing somewhere else.

I reflect on the sheer amount of words they produce – the billions of thoughts that invade the invisible hyper-connected sphere, the Twitter messages and Facebook posts that absorb them completely. Despite this intense exchange of thoughts, words and feelings, they seem to pay no attention to their surroundings. Their minds entranced, computing a never-ending data flow that buzzes by in their digital reality, until a car horn breaks the virtual stream... but awakening just a few, as they blindly attempt to cross the street.

En route to my hotel, I am delighted to see a renovated bookshop and as I pause to browse the newly released titles, I become aware of a large sign that indicates the current popular books. To my pleasure, a large portion of them are 'brain-related'; and there are plenty to choose from! Some of the topics include: the brain in love; the brain and nutrition; the brain in business, the three brains and so forth.

I look at the other shelves, they are filled with countless novels; newly popular erotic fiction titles that now sell like hot cakes; 'Dummies' guides of all kinds; books on how to be a billionaire, build an empire and of course, lose weight. My interest increases as I watch people flock towards the shelves that contain the 'brain books' and I can't help becoming a little excited. There is no doubt that more people have become interested in learning about the brain, particularly as more careers become focused on the abilities of our minds, not our hands. Even when we stroll down the streets aimlessly, we are captured by this growing movement in the simplest of places, such as a humble bookshop.

This frenzy doesn't end here; even US President Barack Obama announced in 2013, a significant investment in the 'Brain Mapping Project', an undertaking that endeavours to help neuroscientists to continue unravelling the mysteries of the pinkish-greyish jelly-like organ inside our skulls. As a biologist and leadership specialist, I continue to be attracted to these new findings about the brain. I know I am not alone in wanting to keep up to date with the latest research.

There is a big community of leadership consultants, therapists, doctors and neuroscientists from all around the world, who are relentlessly experimenting and making new discoveries in this realm.

UNFORGETTABLE MANDELA

While writing this book, Nelson Mandela, at age 94, was admitted to hospital suffering from a serious lung infection. I took some time to reflect on what kind of leader he has been throughout his lifetime – certainly one of the most admired in the world.

I am convinced he had a beautiful and balanced brain. A brain which allowed him to adapt to unexpected circumstances and maintain serenity in moments of distress and chaos. A brain that had probably enjoyed more optimistic than pessimistic thoughts, and that remained focused on his main purpose despite the obstacles along the way.

UK Prime Minister Gordon Brown once described Mandela as "the biggest and most courageous of all leaders from this generation of politicians." Mandela's high regard of self allowed him to pursue his vision while tolerating prosecution, torture, prison, criticism and marriage dissolution. I wonder what made him the greatest...

When reading through a blog post by one of my co-authors, Spanish leadership guru Juan Carlos Cubeiro, I discovered a passage he wrote about the three key traits Mandela possessed;

- Respect for others.

- An incredible talent to make everyone around him feel that they are exceptional individuals – better than they think they are.

- Dedication to humanity beyond his own interests.

It would not surprise me if the 27 years Mandela spent in jail acted as an unparalleled opportunity for him to re-frame his thoughts and negative emotions, and probably rewire his neural connections towards a healthier brain state.

Mandela came out of prison speaking of forgiveness and reconciliation. He was able to manage his mind and keep the focus on how to help South Africa get out of the apartheid system of racial segregation.

I only wish brain imaging technology had been available at the time of Mandela's imprisonment and subsequent release. We may then have had the opportunity to learn and understand what happened to this unique brain of his.

As I write, an interview on television depicts a 12-year-old South African boy who speaks passionately about "Madiba" (Mandela's nickname in his native tribe's language).

The boy says ⊕

"He is a great leader, he cares about people and I love him."

I don't believe anybody can, or will ever be like Mandela, as everybody is unique and every brain is different.

However, if "respect for others" is one of the main traits he is remembered for, I have no hesitation in saying that a loving state of being and a mindful brain have been the main assets Mandela was able to develop in order to cause such significant impact on others – probably without even knowing it.

So, while no one can be like Mandela (or any other leader you admire),
you may be asking... ⊕

CAN PEOPLE IMPROVE THEIR LEADERSHIP?
THE ANSWER IS YES. ABSOLUTELY, YES.

LEADERSHIP IN ACTION

Throughout my career, I have seen hundreds of people transform and discover qualities they didn't know they had – some of them occupied positions of importance, while others were just the 'average' person performing a managerial role.

I have seen individuals become more patient, less angry, more effective and more caring. I have watched them increase their levels of consciousness as they started to experience a more fulfilled and satisfied existence.

In the business world however, many so-called 'leaders' not only lack the ability to inspire, but also the knowledge required to create a system that provides a nurturing environment in which people feel encouraged and supported to perform at their best.

This causes both confusion and uncertainty and consequently, workplaces become toxic – hence the term 'toxic bosses', which has recently grown so much in popularity that there are entire books and blogs dedicated to it, even though they have always existed.

Toxic bosses can be easily identified by traits which include:

- Being condescending

- Never taking time to listen

- Treating others poorly

They usually don't know and rarely ask how they come across to others. They are often blind with regards to how their behaviours, manners and procedures can impact the performance and emotional health of the people they interact with.

To illustrate this point, here are two examples of 'leaders' from the corporate world who occupied significantly different positions, however in both cases, these 'leaders' had the power to influence others.

The first is a true story, about a 21-year-old woman working for a call centre in Australia. I have used a fictional name (Belinda) to protect her identity. The second one is about the CEO of a big financial institution; a real-life character from the book and movie with the same title, "Too Big to Fail" written by Andrew Ross Sorkin.

CASE 1: NAME & SHAME

Belinda is the daughter of a friend of mine. She had been working for a call centre in the heart of the city for approximately 6 months.

One day she came home from work, extremely disillusioned with her job after experiencing issues with her manager. When I was approached by her father who asked me to talk with her, I was astonished at the content of one of the emails she had received that same day. What was more disturbing was to know that this email was a common work tactic utilised by her manager on a weekly basis.

Belinda gave me her permission for some of the content to be published in this book. To someone in my line of work, the outcomes of this tactic are: disengaged employees, low morale and reduced productivity. I would like to share it with you, so you can form your own opinion.

Hi team,

It seems that while some of you have been paying attention to the fact we have emails that need doing, some of you are being pretty lazy about it.

There is NO reason that **ANYONE's** occupancy should NOT be above the 85% target**.

YOU need to pull your socks up **IMMEDIATELY** or you can sit in a room with me and explain why you think it's fair your teammates work hard and you don't.

Hint — you won't enjoy this conversation or the consequences! I am sick of having to remind people about this!!!

Name and shame:
Belinda*, Paula*, Suzie*, Lindy* and Daniel*

* Names have been changed for privacy reasons
** The occupancy rate in question was above 80% for most of the employees (the table showing all the statistics was attached to the original email).

Belinda attempted to speak to her manager to clarify the issue, but was turned away several times. The manager's excuse was that 'she had lots on her plate' and did not have time for a one-on-one.

Feeling both rejected and undermined in front of her colleagues affected Belinda's levels of confidence and her desire to work for the company and for this particular manager. She decided to resign.

Even though the prospect of looking for a new job meant being out of cash for a few months, Belinda took this option, rather than continuing to work at a place where she felt ignored and humiliated.

I know Belinda well – she is a smart girl, efficient and always willing to learn. She is young and has favourable circumstances that allowed her to make the choice of looking for another job. Unfortunately, this is not the case for all who may find themselves in a similar situation.

After she resigned, I phoned to ask her the main reasons for her departure, to which she responded... ⊕

THERE IS NO RESPECT FOR PEOPLE AND I FEEL TOTALLY IGNORED. THE ONLY THING THIS MANAGER CARES ABOUT IS ACHIEVING HER GOALS AND KEY PERFORMANCE INDICATORS (KPIs).

SHE IS NEVER AVAILABLE TO LISTEN TO ANYONE AND IT SEEMS THAT THE ONLY THING THAT MATTERS IS TO LOOK GOOD IN FRONT OF THE CEO OF THE COMPANY.

A 21 year old employee at a call centre

CASE 2: TOO BIG TO FAIL

This case study is based on real-life characters from the book (and adapted movie with the same title) "Too Big To Fail", written by Andrew Ross Sorkin. The story is about the biggest bankruptcy in history and even though the dialogues in the movie may have been invented, the film itself was based on actual events and public record.

In September 2008, the world witnessed the collapse of big financial institutions. This affected the lives of millions of people and led to direct intervention by the US government. Funds were injected into the financial system and the government 'bailed out' a number of banks to avoid an economic disaster.

At the time, decisions had to be made by the CEOs of the major banks and also by government officials such as the US Secretary of the Treasury Henry Paulson. "Too Big to Fail" documents all of the personal conversations and negotiations between some of the most powerful men and women in the USA and recounts tales of greed, envy, arrogance and obsession with power.

In one of the film's first scenes, a journalist is reporting on Lehman Brothers CEO Richard Fuld's leadership. The handling of his company's affairs is being questioned by the public following a 45% drop in the price of the company's stock in a single day.

Fuld is shown as someone who is overly impatient, stressed and mainly concerned about the $90 million he personally lost. His arrogance, self-centred actions, lack of control and sarcastic approach to those who could have helped him ruin any possibility of saving the organisation and avoiding further damage to the economy.

Many of the scenes in this film depict issues and challenges for the leaders at the top of powerful organisations. It is time to re-assess what type of leaders are chosen to occupy these critical positions and what development and feedback they need in order to make more balanced decisions. After all, they have the power to affect the lives of many.

It doesn't take much to realise that to run a billion-dollar business or bank, those at the top need to be smart, understand the 'numbers' and have the level of resilience required to cope with the demands and expectations of many stakeholders.

But... is this all that matters? Aren't we selecting the same people with the same attitudes or behaviours and keeping them at the top without offering any development to keep their brains in balance?

I wonder if it is even possible for CEOs to display the serenity, respect and social abilities that people admire so much in a leader.

With some exceptions, leaders are expected to demonstrate a completely different set of values and behaviours to what they usually display. With a leadership style very different to the one that people admire in a leader (Mandela's style), I ask the question:

Do these business leaders have the capacity to reflect on what they are doing, and realise how important it is to model the right behaviours for the rest of the people in their organisations?

Undoubtedly, the gap between what actually happens and people's expectations is big and not easy to close. A scary reality is that many responsible and intelligent leaders, even with the best information at hand, can be biased in the assessment of a situation when making critical decisions.

Combining a person's biases with limited self-awareness can result in a leaders' actions looking very disappointing, particularly when decisions turn out to be the wrong ones.

These two case studies are only a small window into what occurs in many workplaces around the world. Despite incessant references to the importance of leadership, there is a pervading sense that people in positions of power just don't seem to care enough to make the personal changes, which are essential to good leadership.

Perhaps the current pace of life is compelling us to become less caring, resulting in our attention only being focused on the things that provide us with immediate rewards. Or maybe, our brains cannot deal with such complex, uncertain and demanding work practices, while at the same time, being caring, supportive and empathetic.

ONE THING THAT IS EVIDENT IS
THAT 'THINKING BEYOND SELF'
OCCUPIES THE BACK SEAT IN THE MINDS
OF MANY LEADERS, WHEN THERE ARE
MORE PRESSING DEMANDS.

THE MINDFULNESS ERA

Increasing self-awareness and developing a mindful brain are two of the trendiest topics in the fields of leadership, coaching, therapy and neuroscience today.

One of the world's experts on the subject of mindfulness is Harvard psychologist and professor Dr. Ellen Langer. The notion of 'mindfulness' has several meanings and is not an easy concept to define. One definition explains 'mindfulness' as ⊕

"The capacity to bring one's complete attention to the present experience in a non-judgemental way."

According to Dr. Langer, being mindful carries with it some great benefits including:

- Becoming more sensitive to our environment.

- Being more open to new information.

- Becoming more aware of multiple perspectives when solving problems.

In addition to being mindful, Dr. Langer also states that ⊕

"Focusing on the gift of re-framing the small things that make us feel annoyed can have a significant impact in reducing stress levels, helping us lead healthier and happier lives."

The "re-framing" Langer refers to, consists of changing the way we see things and finding an alternative view, in regards to the events or situations that we experience. While it is a relatively simple concept, it is very common to see people becoming stuck in their own viewpoints with no ability to change them.

A useful theory that was originally formulated in the 1980s by John Grinder and Judith Delozier — as part of the discipline called Neuro-Linguistic Programming (NLP) — defines this process of getting 'caught up' in our own views, as being in first position.

When we are in first position, our viewpoint is subjective and we become absorbed by our emotions. This results in unreasonable reactions to any stimulus that upsets us. In this position, we only see the world through our eyes, which can be useful to reflect about what we learn, our inner experiences and feelings.

However, it is the least useful position from which we should engage when developing relations with others or in dealing with emotional or confronting situations.

In first position, we are only interested in expressing what we think, how we feel or our opinions. Active listening and respect for what others have to say is important in almost every situation, and they can easily become impossible tasks if we only pay attention to the thoughts and feelings we are experiencing.

With the accelerated lives we live today, we are constantly bombarded and distracted by large volumes of information and sounds from our devices. Our lack of time and patience for others' issues is in complete opposition to what is required if we want to 're-frame'.

'Re-framing' requires slowing down and the willingness to look at a situation through the eyes of the other person. This is known as second position in NLP.

In the world of business and leadership, it is not unusual to see people running their teams and organisations from first position, which causes major problems to those around them. When people get stuck mainly on what they want, they are usually perceived as egotistical, self-centred and insensitive.

Looking back at the Mandela example, it appears that living in the world without any consideration for other people's ideas, thoughts or feelings is exactly the opposite to the behavioural make-up of a great leader.

Findings presented last year by Dr. Matthew Lieberman (Neuroscientist, UCLA), provide a good explanation for why 'busy people' are likely to be less observant, attentive and respectful of others. Lieberman explains how our ability to 'mentalise' – that is thinking about others or predicting other people's emotional or intentional states -requires effort, attention and considerable brain resources.

His research demonstrates the reduced ability that people who are extremely busy and stressed at work have when they need to consider what others are thinking, or what others may need (second position).

Second position is about imagining what it is like to be another person. If our ability to consider other people's thoughts is poor, even when we are not under pressure, then it is not difficult to conclude that if we want to become a centred, well-balanced leader who is able to influence others, increasing our level of attention and energy towards people is just as important as getting the job done.

Lieberman also suggests that those who spend most of their time analysing and focusing on goals and strategies are turning off the social circuits that allow them to think about others. If we couple this with the difficulty that exists to think about the minds of others in stressful circumstances, it is understandable why there is an emotional gap between cognitively depleted top level executives and people who know how to lead well.

This is only the tip of the iceberg when attempting to understand the brain and how its lack of balance may affect individual performance, self-control, decision-making and consequently a person's leadership ability.

It is quite astonishing that we have disregarded the incredible organ inside our skull for such a long time, when in reality our choices, behaviours, emotions, decisions, actions and so on depend on what happens inside our brains.

Now that we are beginning to gather valuable information, it would be even more astonishing if leaders and organisations ignored the root cause of what can help us become successful or can lead to our demise.

It's time for our brains to collectively work together.

ON NEUROLEADERSHIP AND NEUROLEADERS

At a neuroleadership conference in Los Angeles, I was seated behind one of the pioneers and gurus of the contemporary field of leadership, Warren Bennis.

I observed his actions as he sat quietly, paying attention to every word that neuroscientist Dr. Naomi Eisenberg uttered. On this occasion, Eisenberg was presenting on how the brain responds to 'social pain' – that being how humans react when feeling excluded, ostracised or disconnected from others.

As she delivered her presentation, Bennis (who is now in his eighties) impatiently raised his hand and asked her a question, to which she responded in a beautiful way explaining her point. Bennis then stood up, gazed out over the crowd of 250 consultants and experts and said ⊕

"I wish I would have known all of this when I started to write and teach leadership 60 years ago."

Over the past 60 years, there have certainly been many leadership gurus and many competencies, qualities and skills that have been defined and redefined. I could mention an array of other experts, but for now, let's look at some of the leadership qualities Bennis mentions in his work. He refers to six personal qualities that anyone who wants to lead should focus on developing:

- Integrity

- Dedication

- Creativity

- Magnanimity

- Openness

- Humility

Most people would agree that these qualities make sense and that they are the type of traits that everyone wants to see in a leader.

For many years, organisations have searched for and developed rating systems of specific traits without understanding that the development of a leader is highly correlated with the development and optimisation of the leader's brain.

However, this is rapidly changing and many of the theories and frameworks developed around leadership are becoming obsolete as more research about the brain emerges.

In an article entitled "The Economy of the Neuroleader", which I authored in January 2012 (published by Australian magazine *HR Daily*), I referred to the importance of recruiting and developing 'Neuroleaders', instead of selecting and promoting people based only on their technical expertise and business acumen.

Promoting leaders based on technical competencies has been the primary driver over the past few decades. Most organisations are filled with managers who prefer to focus on numbers and investment returns, rather than on people — a tactic that is no longer viable in our ever-changing society.

In the eyes of many experts, business schools and MBA programs have largely failed to develop the leadership characteristics and skills that are necessary for organisations to succeed in a future that requires agility, collaboration and innovation.

These competencies are not just 'nice to have'. They are an imperative for survival.

Over the past hundred years, the education system has also focused on academic performance, with the development of self and social awareness being ignored. The outcomes of this lack of development are people in positions of power not knowing how to be self-aware (knowing self) nor socially aware (knowing how to relate to others). Having an emphasis on numbers and profits is important for a business to succeed, but having leaders who only use this way of thinking without knowing how to take care of the human capital leads to the inevitable stagnation of the organisation.

We are experiencing economic, social and business transformations that require the development of mindsets and skills which support leadership in a new way.

In my experience, it seems that positional power is being replaced by the capacity to inspire and the ability to create emotional connections with people from different teams, cultures and generations.

Furthermore, social media is strongly driving this phenomenon of 'anyone can be a leader', as it is now easier for anyone who has something to say and knows how to communicate to gather a following. Although individuals are able to respond to trends faster than large organisations, it would be a disadvantage for well-established companies to remain on the sidelines of this phenomenon.

Successfully navigating this constantly changing business climate requires leaders who can learn to think about others in order to engage them in the most effective and positive way.

However, leading to engage others is not enough – leaders need to invest half their time in 'leading themselves'.

Employers have an opportunity, therefore, to rethink how they develop their leaders and include the brain as part of this new approach to leadership. While it is hard to believe that the organ that makes us decide, think, prioritise and perceive others has been ignored for so long; we now have emerging leadership models that will give rise to a new age of 'neuroleaders'. My definition for "Neuroleader" is the following:

A 'Neuroleader' is someone who first leads self by understanding his/her brain functioning and strives to optimise its performance.

The concept of 'NeuroLeadership' was first coined in 2006 by Dr. David Rock, a leadership consultant, visionary businessman and Director of the NeuroLeadership Institute – a global initiative that brings neuroscientists and leadership experts together to build a new science for leadership development.

Memorable to many in the industry was Dr. Rock's 2009 statement that... ➔

THE ABILITY TO INTENTIONALLY ADDRESS THE SOCIAL BRAIN IN THE SERVICE OF OPTIMAL PERFORMANCE WILL BE A DISTINGUISHING LEADERSHIP CAPABILITY IN THE YEARS AHEAD.

Dr. David Rock

Despite some leadership and coaching experts still being in doubt that 'brain-centred leadership' is the correct approach, and others arguing that neuroscientific studies currently underway may not be relevant enough, it is quite remarkable what Dr. Rock has achieved by organising the Neuroleadership Summits.

These summits act as a place where people from different disciplines can come together and have open dialogues. It is refreshing to see an environment where neuroscientists are able to inform business people on the workings of the brain and their research experiments; while organisational leaders, consultants and human resource practitioners discuss their views, explore challenges and brainstorm on the possible applications of this knowledge. This, in itself, is an example of collaboration in action.

We now have valuable information regarding the functioning of the brain that we did not have before; and the majority of people I have encountered are fascinated when this topic gets taught and explored at leadership programs and conferences.

The brain is at the centre of what we do, the decisions we make, our behaviours, common sense, emotions and leadership abilities; so it seems very reasonable to let go of what we knew before and open our eyes to the new knowledge we are being presented with, accepting that it is, like ourselves, a work in progress.

While the concept of Neuroleaders continues to grow and change every day, it is definitely something we should embrace rather than be afraid of.

With this thought, I would like to conclude with two compelling pieces from a blog post on 'The emergence of the Neuroleader' (written by Laurie Ellington and Paul McFadden from Zero Point Leadership, published in November 2012). ⊕

NEUROLEADERS ARE CONSCIOUS THAT THE GROUNDWORK VITAL TO ACCESSING HUMAN POTENTIAL AND EXPANDING TALENT IN ANY ORGANISATION OR SYSTEM IS SELF-EXPANSION.

THEY HOLD A MENTAL MODEL FOR INTEGRATION AND GROWTH, POSSESS THE ABILITY TO LINK AND ARE ABLE TO SEE THE INTELLIGENCE IN THE WHOLE VERSUS PARTS; AND MUST ULTIMATELY BE ABLE TO INSPIRE OTHERS TO DO THE SAME.

AS WE BRING HARD SCIENCE TO THE FOREFRONT OF HUMAN PERFORMANCE OPTIMISATION, WE SEE THE NEUROLEADER BEGINNING TO SURFACE, EVOLVING A NEW LEADERSHIP ARCHETYPE – ONE THAT ATTRACTS PEOPLE TO CHANGE SYSTEMICALLY INSTEAD OF MECHANISTICALLY, INSPIRING OTHERS TO IMMERSE THEMSELVES IN LOOKING BELOW THE SURFACE TO INVESTIGATE WHAT HONESTLY ADVANCES HUMAN FUNCTIONING AND POSITIVE CHANGE IN OURSELVES, OUR ORGANISATIONS AND OUR COMMUNITIES.

Laurie Ellington and Paul McFadden

Chapter Three

THE WOMAN AFTER NEXT OR WOMEN NEXT?

THERE'S SOMETHING ABOUT JULIA

After a brief and very turbulent time as Australia's first female Prime Minister (2010 – 2013), Julia Gillard declared during an emotional farewell that, "It will be easier for the next woman and I am proud of that".

Listening to Gillard express that it will be easier for the next woman is a clear statement that things are currently not easy for the female gender. Meanwhile in the Sydney Morning Herald, Tanja Kovac was writing: ⊕

"While in her speech, Gillard was ambivalent about the impact gender had on her rise and fall, men and women from across the country acknowledged the impact of an underlying sexism, even misogyny, on her leadership."

Far from being a political commentator and without any intention of making any political statement, discussing Gillard's case is a good starting point to look into the assumptions, ideals and expectations that most of us hold in regards to what a leader should or should not do.

Being a political figure takes courage and being the first of any group even more so, but being a leader who has to do the job well and at the same time battle against covert opinions and behaviours can be exceptionally intimidating.

When a person feels intimidated, their brain's threat response activates and consequently they are less likely to be able to express their true potential.

Deep in our hearts, we all know this, and looking at the statistics, there is a clear demonstration of inequality at the top. In the next few pages, there are a few of them which are widely mentioned when people talk about inequality.

WHEN A PERSON FEELS INTIMIDATED,
THEIR BRAIN'S THREAT RESPONSE
ACTIVATES AND CONSEQUENTLY THEY
ARE LESS LIKELY TO BE ABLE TO EXPRESS
THEIR TRUE POTENTIAL.

~

IN 2013
ONLY **23** OF THE
FORTUNE **500** CEOs
WERE WOMEN.

Source: www.catalyst.org

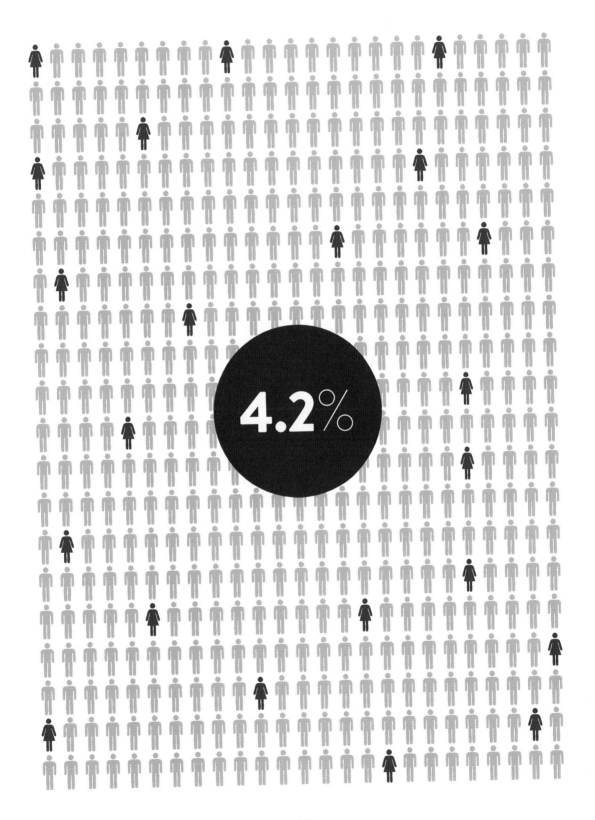

4.2%

WOMEN BOARD CHAIRS

Source: www.catalyst.org

~

19%
OF **EQUITY PARTNERS**
IN THE 50 BEST
LAW FIRMS ARE WOMEN.

Source: www.catalyst.org

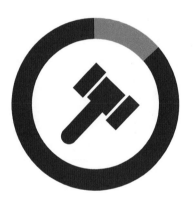

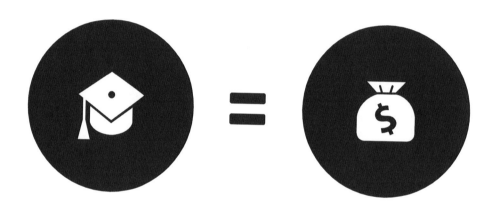

~

IN AMERICA
FEMALE GRADUATES'
STARTING SALARIES ARE
$5000 LESS PER YEAR
THAN THEIR MALE
COUNTERPARTS.

Source: www.catalyst.org

UNCONSCIOUS BIAS

In the "Gender Equality Project" report, published by the "Centre for Ethical Leadership" (part of Melbourne Business School) in November 2012, the authors stated that "women who aspire to leadership and other male-dominated occupations carry a heavy and hidden handicap due to unconscious bias."

In comparison with their male peers, women are rated lower, regardless of whether they behave in a stereotypically masculine or feminine way. These evaluation penalties include being assessed as less likeable than male peers who display the same behaviour and less competent at their work than their male peers who perform at the same level. These negative evaluations of women relative to men are more pronounced in male-dominated occupations.

Although these unconscious biases exist, the participation of women in economic growth cannot be denied.

WOMEN ARE MUCH MORE LIKELY THAN MEN TO SAY THAT THE TWO GENDERS ARE NOT TREATED EQUALLY.

WOMEN ARE UNITED IN THEIR VIEWS ACROSS GENERATIONS: MILLENNIAL WOMEN, WHO ARE STARTING THEIR CAREERS ON FAIRLY EQUAL FOOTING WITH THEIR MALE COUNTERPARTS, ARE JUST AS LIKELY AS OLDER GENERATIONS TO BELIEVE THAT WOMEN FACE AN UPHILL BATTLE, IN TERMS OF BEING TREATED EQUALLY BY SOCIETY AND BY EMPLOYERS.

US Pew Research Center

JUST LEANING IN?

It is also true, that there are women all around the world who achieve high levels of success in their own right.

Such is the case of Sheryl Sandberg, Facebook's COO and author of the book "Lean In." Although she agrees with the fact that there are invisible barriers for women's advancement, she also has another view on the matter, stating a few times throughout her book that women are the ones who sabotage themselves by lacking self-confidence and pulling back when they should be leaning in. According to Sandberg, this is the reason why "men still run the world".

At this point, I will deliberately stop myself from joining the critics who have commented on Sandberg's views, as in my opinion, someone who does something different and in support of others should be applauded rather than criticised.

I would like to believe that this is Sandberg's true intention, considering her track record, degrees, prestige and wealth that back up her initiative: the "Lean In" Circles. Quite possibly, she will be remembered as someone who has significantly contributed to easing the way for women who work in current and future workplaces. Although saying that women lack self-confidence and developing educational programs does not solve the problem in its totality, it is a great beginning. The question in my mind is:

Why is there an epidemic of low self-confidence among the female population? What causes it? Does it occur in every environment or in the face of strong opinions and competitive/power driven behaviours, where the female voice gets lost amid the louder ones in the room?

Having had the opportunity to witness and listen to many highly intelligent professional women express their inability to articulate their views in open meetings led by peers who often don't listen or continuously undermine their ideas or suggestions, I am quite certain that if the same women were placed in a different setting where they felt better supported, they would be able to express themselves without feeling unsure of the validity of their perspectives.

Based on years of observing people interact in meetings and training programs, the way that women seem to prefer to express themselves (ideas, opinions, issues and associated feelings) is by sharing them openly with those who are willing to listen and can offer acknowledgement or support when needed.

When both of these essential communication elements are not present, women either withhold their contributions and become passive, or they feel they have to make their point more overtly by speaking louder or gesticulating to match the tone and pace of the other person. In this case, some women tend to experience a divide between who they really are and who they feel they have to be in order to be heard.

ON COMMUNICATION & EMOTIONS

Australian researcher Dr. Margaret Byrne based her PhD work filming men and women in 28 different workplaces to evaluate how each gender deals with each other in a number of situations, including one-on-one meetings, team meetings and performance appraisal situations. Her interview can be found on YouTube.

In the case of team meetings, she was able to capture and analyse the interactions in:

- Men-only meetings

- Women-only meetings

- Mixed meetings

Dr. Byrne believes that meetings are the 'arena' which women need to conquer if they are to progress in their professional careers. She says that 95% of the time, men and women display similar communication patterns, however, it is the remaining 5% that creates the frustration that people experience when dealing with the opposite sex in the workplace.

According to Dr. Byrne, the gold standard is still set by how men interact when attending a work meeting. For example, men go into a meeting with an idea or solution to a problem which they have mulled over and present the solution with absolute confidence. They will get straight to the point and offer an idea that has already been worked out in their minds without needing further improvement.

In contrast, when women want to talk about an idea, they start sharing it in its embryonic state with others around them (in women-only meetings) often laughing, while talking in overlapping conversations to flesh it out.

In mixed meetings, Dr. Byrne says women have no opportunity to flesh their ideas out. I imagine this may happen because men either lack the patience or the willingness to listen to an unfinished idea. This biological bias can be seen throughout evolution, as men (the hunters) were required to compete with one another, while women (the gatherers) found a greater need for collaboration. Interestingly, this bias still seems to be present today.

This is not to say that women cannot put their points across in a direct way or that some men don't want to discuss their thoughts and ideas with their collaborators. But it seems that communication for women operates on different levels, for example: the need to discover the best idea in conjunction with others and to use verbal communication as a coping mechanism for stressful situations.

The conclusions from Dr. Byrne's work are extremely important to take into account if we want to focus on the needs to be addressed, instead of getting caught in the negative emotions that may arise due to the variations in communication styles.

Having had the opportunity to test some of these findings myself in the context of leadership and emotional intelligence programs, where people are asked to share personal experiences, I have noticed significant distinctions when it comes to disclosing feelings and showing vulnerabilities.

Below are some of my observations in the case of mixed groups:

- Women are more cautious expressing how they feel or sharing their personal stories when members of the opposite sex are present. However, once a level of trust is established, they don't hesitate to open up to the group and freely say what they want to say.

- Men, in general, take longer than women to loosen up and share feelings and stories, with many struggling to find the words to describe their emotions. In most cases, men's emotional vocabulary is more limited.

- Some men are hesitant or unsure about how to ask questions or share something that may be considered borderline between professional and personal, particularly with their female counterparts.

- There are varying degrees of discomfort among male participants in terms of listening and expressing feelings. Those who spend 2-3 days practicing 'emotional disclosure' and learning 'how to be vulnerable', leave the workshops with a renewed perspective on how to better connect with people at work (including their female colleagues).

In the case of female-only groups:

- Women are much more eloquent when given the opportunity. They enjoy talking openly about their feelings and speaking about their work issues.

- It seems unnecessary to create an environment where women can feel safe for them to initiate a conversation on personal or work matters, since they naturally do this.

- When a woman shares a gloomy or sad story, the rest of the group jumps in to acknowledge and offer a kind and comforting word without hesitation. It is quite well-known that women are naturally good at understanding facial expressions, an ability that undoubtedly helps them to assess how others may be feeling and provide support if they deem this to be appropriate.

In the last 5 to 10 years, talking about emotions in the workplace has become popular (even normal), and as leaders start to understand that emotions cannot be left at the door, they become interested in the strategies that can be used to enhance their emotional capabilities.

Women seem to have tapped into the emotional intelligence concept rapidly. Men, however, are also opening up to participate in this type of development, probably influenced by the female interest.

This is a growing trend and I can see the significant impact it is having on how we understand and deal with each other's emotions when we make decisions, engage with one another, communicate and lead.

THE BRAIN & GENDER

While the roles that men and women play in society today have changed in comparison to those performed in the past, our brains and hormonal systems have not shifted at the same pace.

Ever since scientists were first able to look inside people's brains and started seeing correlations between scan results and a person's actions or responses, many researchers and commentators around the world (scientists and non-scientists) have proposed their own arguments to either support or dismiss the new knowledge emerging from such studies.

Some are so adamant in making the point that brain-gender difference research studies will only contribute even more to the gender inequality issue, that I am quite reticent to add any of my own conclusions on this matter.

There are plenty of books written on this topic and I have selected a few of the latest research findings that may potentially aid those who have to lead and work with men and women. In my opinion, if we are to create more effective and harmonious workplaces, we need to educate ourselves on how to apply these findings about gender differences in the brain and the leadership and communication preferences that emerge from them.

We are heading towards a more collaborative society where both men and women and their capacities will start to be better understood, accepted and valued. Learning more about the resources we count on at a biological level should not cause fear, but rather facilitate understanding.

Firstly, I'd like to refer to the work of Dr. Daniel Amen, renowned American neuropsychiatric, brain imaging specialist and best-selling author, who has performed more than 83,000 brain scans. He wrote a book specifically addressing the female brain called "Unleashing the Power of the Female Brain" published in 2013.

One of the reasons for writing this book was his belief in the enormous difference women make to family life, teams, businesses and society. From my perspective, Dr. Amen's work forms part of the newest body of evidence when it comes to brain imaging findings and that is why I decided to have my brain scanned at one of his clinics in America, with the aim of better understanding my brain and satisfy my own curiosity.

For those who want to learn more, there is a wealth of useful information in his book, which I highly recommend.

The table below summarises some key gender differences in the brain and how they may impact people's behaviours. ⊕

BRAIN DIFFERENCES	BEHAVIOURS
Compared to males, females have more grey matter in the regions of the brain's mirror neuron system.	Higher levels of empathy, which facilitate forming an emotional connection with others.
The amygdala (the part of the brain that processes fear) is bigger in men.	Responsible for triggering aggression and action, stimulating competitiveness.
The hippocampus (the centre for learning, memory and emotion) is larger and more active in the female brain.	Women tend to have better memory when it comes to details associated with emotional events, but it is also more difficult to erase emotional memories.
The prefrontal cortex (part of the frontal lobe and responsible for controlling anger, among other functions) matures earlier and is larger in women than in men.	This allows women to keep strong negative emotions in check. They exhibit better self-control, are less impulsive and are willing to compromise if they need to, even at their own expense.
Compared to women, when making decisions under stress, men have more activation in the reward circuits of the brain.	It appears that men will be motivated to act more quickly, while women tend to wait until the stressful situation has passed (less activation of the reward system).
The anterior cingulate gyrus (the part of the brain that helps you shift attention and recognise errors) is more active in women than in men, which makes their brains 'busier'.	Women will not stop worrying.
Women's centres of language are bigger and more active in both sides of the brain.	Women can be more expressive and eloquent and do better in tasks that involve the use of language.
Men have larger parietal lobes while women have thicker areas in this part of the brain.	Men are able to represent a shape and rotate objects mentally better than women.

Source: Unleash the Power of the Female Brain, Dr. Daniel Amen (2013) www.amenclinics.com

In addition to Dr. Amen's insights about brain differences, other studies, such as the Neural Mapping report published in the Proceedings of the National Academy of Sciences Journal (2013), by Ragini Verma (University of Pennsylvania) are also worth mentioning.

These neural maps have appeared from one of the largest studies looking at how brains are wired in healthy males and females using a technique called diffusion tensor imaging, which mapped the neural connections of 1,000 participants (429 males and 571 females).

Verma was able to confirm that significant differences exist in the wiring of male and female brains, with the maps showing that women's brains are more suited to social and intuitive skills, memory and multi-tasking, due to greater connectivity between the left and right side of the brain. Men's brains are better suited to spatial skills and coordination, with their connections more confined to individual hemispheres, except in the case of the cerebellum.

The work of American anthropologist and human behaviour researcher Dr. Helen Fisher, a leading expert on the biology of relationships, may also shed some light into how both genders' chemistry can influence leadership traits and behaviours.

As she describes it, women are comfortable when they are able to talk to each other and engage in eye-to-eye interaction, the 'anchoring gaze', as she calls it. Men on the other hand, can enjoy each other's company by simply being side to side and not saying a word while watching a good football game. Problems arise when a woman wants to be looked at, while she is talking, and the man is looking away (and in his mind, this is absolutely fine).

Even though Dr. Fisher refers to love and friendship relationships between genders, I believe this is an important point to consider also in working relationships.

Have you ever felt ignored by colleagues whom you want to talk to, but they are not engaging in the way you expect? Do they keep looking at their computer or doing something else while you are trying to have a conversation?

HORMONAL SYSTEMS

According to Dr. Fisher, this behaviour may be linked to the hormones and neurotransmitters that our brains and bodies produce.

There are four systems that seem to have a significant influence on how we function as human beings, and even though we all have these chemicals, there is a predominance of one over the other based on gender (in the case of testosterone/estrogen). Interestingly though, there seems to be no gender-related difference in the case of the dopamine/serotonin systems.

The four systems are:

- **The Estrogen/Oxytocin System**
  This gives women (and some men) the ability to observe, intuit, talk more, bond and foster connections with others. Women prefer a win-win approach and tend to assign more value to collaborating with others rather than competing. More women than men express the estrogen/oxytocin system.

- **The Testosterone System**
  This gives men (and some women) the ability to be direct, decisive, analytical and focused. People with high levels of testosterone are more inclined to give and take orders, follow rules, compete and win. Many more men express the testosterone system and have 10 to 100 times more testosterone than women.

- **The Dopamine System**
  People whose brains produce more dopamine (and the accompanying substance nor-epinephrine) are very curious, enthusiastic, optimistic, spontaneous and impulsive. They may be inclined to associate themselves with other 'high dopamine' individuals.

- **The Serotonin System**
  People whose brains produce more serotonin are more cautious (but not fearful), calm, loyal, self-controlled, frugal and structured. They may be predisposed to associate themselves with other 'high serotonin' individuals. Men produce 52% more serotonin than women and a lack of serotonin can lead to depression, which is the reason why women experience more depression than men.

For those who are interested to know more about these systems, Dr. Helen Fisher's talk is available on YouTube .

In 1989, Dr. Anne Moir, co-author of the book "Brain Sex" said ⊕

MEN AND WOMEN ARE EQUAL ONLY IN THEIR COMMON MEMBERSHIP OF THE SAME SPECIE, HUMANKIND.

THE SEXES ARE DIFFERENT BECAUSE THEIR BRAINS ARE DIFFERENT. THE BRAIN, THE CHIEF ADMINISTRATIVE AND EMOTIONAL ORGAN OF LIFE, IS DIFFERENTLY CONSTRUCTED IN MEN AND IN WOMEN; IT PROCESSES INFORMATION IN A DIFFERENT WAY, WHICH RESULTS IN DIFFERENT PERCEPTIONS, PRIORITIES AND BEHAVIOUR.

Dr. Anne Moir

IT HAS TAKEN MANY YEARS FOR PEOPLE OUTSIDE THE SCIENTIFIC REALM TO START EXPLORING AND DISCUSSING THESE DIFFERENCES, WITHOUT FEELING THEY ARE BEING POLITICALLY INCORRECT.

I AM HOPEFUL THAT THESE CONVERSATIONS WILL HELP MEN AND WOMEN INTERACT WITH EACH OTHER BETTER THAN EVER BEFORE.

IT'S TRUE: WOMEN CAN WORK AND LEAD

The capacity of women to work, achieve and lead is no longer in question, as plenty of research exists showing that companies do better financially when more women are part of their executive teams.

A number of studies performed by different consulting firms in the past five years found that boards with a significant representation of women have a 66% higher return on invested capital, 53% higher return on equity and a 42% higher return on sales compared to boards with more men.

When it comes to the ability to lead, Catalyst, a think tank based in London, undertook a study using a 360-degree competency assessment that aimed to compare how both men and women rated in terms of leadership effectiveness.

The results showed that women achieved better results in 12 of the 16 competencies chosen, with the 360-degree evaluations including bosses, clients, subordinates, colleagues and associates of the candidates, offering their views specifically on these competencies.

It is quite astounding that in 2014, research studies continue to be undertaken to ascertain that women can do great work and also lead, considering that there are so many examples of women accomplishing incredible things throughout the world.

Examples include those who have led causes, such as Ayaa Hirsi Ali, the Somali-born American activist, writer and politician, Dr. Candace Pert, an American neuroscientist and pharmacologist who discovered the opiate receptor and Aung San Suu Kyi, Burmese politician and chairperson for the National League for Democracy, who endured years of house arrest and personal sacrifice to fight for the rights of her fellow citizens.

SOCIETAL CONDITIONS

While it is positive that there are so many examples of exceptional women, it is also true that their chances of success will vary from country to country, depending on the societal conditions.

For example:

- In India, 5.5 million women enter the workforce every year, although 50% report concerns about their safety in relation to commuting, which impact their hours and availability.

- In Tanzania, there are an estimated 720,000 to 1.2 million female entrepreneurs, but because tribal laws dictate that only sons inherit land, women lack the most common collateral for securing loans.

- In Saudi Arabia, 57% of university graduates are women, yet only 12% participate in the workforce.

As I go through these revealing findings from Booz researchers, with their estimations that nearly one billion women will be entering the global economy in the coming decade, I wonder – are we prepared for this to happen? How will this impact the way that everyone leads and follows?

The ideal leader used to be someone who would issue orders and people would do as they were told. Having explored the brain differences in the previous section, it is not surprising that in a male-dominated workforce, this would be the most habitual when it comes to the preferred way of leading.

I would dare to suggest that the preferred leadership style in today's world is one that fosters collaboration and brings out the best in people. In general, women are naturally good at this and as described above, it seems that the time to acknowledge and validate these differences has arrived.

It remains to be seen how this may affect men and their capacity to lead in a female-dominated environment; and what type of mindsets they will need to develop in order to adapt to a different leadership style.

As more men (particularly the millennial group who are now between 18 and 29 years of age) start to juggle professional, home and parenting duties, it is likely that this generation will push for more flexible work arrangements to allow time for family life. This is already happening in some corners of the globe.

Managing men and their potential new requirements will also demand an open and renewed perspective from leaders in organisations to create workplace practices that cater for a new type of man, one who acts differently to the stereotype that still endures in most people's psyches.

With an increasing number of women joining the business and political arenas, and many men opting to have their own businesses, work from home or part-time, the time has come to contemplate gender differences in the same way that we would think about cultural differences.

MOST ORGANISATIONS RECOGNISE
THE NEED TO BE AWARE OF CULTURAL
IDIOSYNCRASIES WHEN DOING BUSINESS
WITH OTHER COUNTRIES, BUT WHEN
IT COMES TO DOING BUSINESS WITH MEN
AND WOMEN, IMPORTANT DIFFERENCES
ARE ALL TOO OFTEN OVERLOOKED.

CAN MENTORING BE THE STEPPING STONE?

Where I grew up, football (soccer) was only a game for boys and it was considered not very feminine for girls to play. So we sat on the sidelines, joyfully cheering for the boys as they played and scored goals.

For much of its history, organised football has been almost exclusively a man's game, but times have changed and it is now widely accepted that girls play football and some are considerably good at it.

THE SOCCER STORY

Under the strong sun of a summer day at school in Madrid, Spain, a 10-year-old girl is unaware that 30 or 40 years ago, girls did not play football.

What she knows for certain is that she wants to play with her friends in the school yard to practice for their Saturday match. To her surprise, the boys occupying the yard don't let the girl and her friends join in.

Together, the girls go to complain to their female teacher who doesn't know how to solve the problem, other than to talk to the boys. Their snappy and short reply is:

"We were here first and WE are playing."

The teacher decides to call the girls' football coach, a 30-year-old entrepreneur and football lover named Alicia. She is available and runs to the school to sort this out.

Her young team needs support so she makes the time to assist them. After all, the Saturday match is very important for the girls. They play for the Real Madrid Junior League.

Alicia stops the boys' match with a hand that demands respect. She then addresses them with a soft but direct demeanour, offering them a ready-made idea that sprung to her mind on the way to the school.

"You can teach the girls how to score goals. The only rules are that you play together and you let them score."

The boys look at each other, shrug their shoulders and with a gesture, invite the girls to join in. The teacher is astonished. They are playing together.

There is something about owning a ball or a piece of yard that, in this case, gives the boys power over the girls. Despite this, the boys also seem to respond to the clear and straightforward request from the coach.

Taking this real example to the arena of business, I wonder if asking directly for what one wants is one of the ways women can best be heard?

While talking to the coach about this incident, the teacher also reinforced the fact that she noticed the boys' willingness to mentor the girls and offer their suggestions. It seemed to make them feel respected.

You may be amused by this analogy, but in my years of corporate experience I have seen this behaviour many times. It seems natural that someone who is occupying a school yard or a boardroom resists others who want to come in and use the same space.

Even though politically and financially it makes sense to have both genders sitting at the table (this has been previously discussed), the first biological and emotional reaction from men would be to deny such intrusion unless someone asks them directly and with authority, or obliges them to do so – such as using 'quotas' to push women to higher ranks – a controversial solution at best.

Asking people to offer their guidance and support through a mentoring process, be it formal or informal, could potentially become a way to facilitate the insertion of women into male-dominated environments. In my view, more synchronised actions to facilitate inclusion are needed to advance women into senior roles faster if we are to reach equality in the near future.

I keep thinking that if I was a small cat and was placed in a cage with lions, even though we are all felines, I would probably feel in a disadvantaged position and the levels of confidence and courage required to live in this cage would be hard to sustain in comparison to the benefits of being associated with the king of the jungle. Telling the cat to develop a non-fear approach and having a chat from time to time would not matter much, as the chances of survival would be minimal.

When I started my research to write this book, I asked female leaders what they believed the specific differences were when it came to running their teams and businesses, in comparison to what they observed their male counterparts do. I met and interviewed many women from different nationalities and levels of experience who occupied very diverse roles.

THE 10 WAYS WOMAN LEAD

I gathered many thoughts, but in the end, there were ten things that seemed to be most common for all of the women I met. These were:

1. **The role of life partners**

   When a woman had a life partner, the partner was always fully supportive and also proud of her career. Not only that, but he/she helped her with family commitments, children and household chores, thus allowing her to have the time to attend to her duties (with the corresponding negotiations when it came to practicalities).

2. **Single women**

   Women who were single or had been previously married did not regret being in leadership positions, although half of them told me they wished they could have enjoyed the company of a supportive partner along the way. Maybe the other half did not openly tell me the same thing and they might have been wishing to be in a similar situation.

3. **At higher levels**

   In the case of female CEOs and senior executives working for large organisations, whilst they felt comfortable working at this level and truly enjoyed the challenge, they found themselves falling short in other areas of their lives. In 40% of the cases, they mentioned they had to change part of who they were to better match the expectations from the board, their male colleagues and other stakeholders.

4. **When running their own businesses**

   The majority of women who owned and ran their own businesses said they were fulfilled and satisfied and did not even mention the need 'to fit in'. Despite working longer hours in most cases, they were able to keep a better balance between work and home (or other activities of interest), as they liked having the autonomy to make their own decisions.

5. **Passion, a key element**

   They all seemed to agree that they excelled at their jobs when they were able to work on something they were good at and passionate about.

6. **The skills**

When it came to the skills that served them well, they emphasised that being able to articulate their thoughts with confidence, understand their intuitive insights and influence others while remaining calm were essential to their success.

7. **Taking care of themselves**

They all worked hard to achieve their goals and didn't mind it, however most agreed that doing something for themselves (like having a massage, playing sports, or spending time with family) was an essential ingredient to help them manage their levels of energy and stress, so they could feel a sense of balance.

8. **Connection with others**

Connecting with people on their team and knowing them personally in terms of values, likes and dislikes was something they considered extremely valuable and devoted the time to do.

9. **Sounding board**

They all mentioned having friends, mentors or coaches (several of them) whom they could talk with, to gain a different perspective on problems at work and in their personal lives.

10. **Networking**

They were all united in their views and agreed that building networks and seeking support from people of influence had assisted them in building their careers and boosting their businesses.

BASED ON WHAT'S BEING DISCUSSED,
I FEEL OBLIGED TO END THIS CHAPTER
WITH SOME STRATEGIES THAT THE MEN
WHO ARE READING THIS BOOK MAY WANT
TO CONSIDER WHEN INTERACTING WITH
THE OPPOSITE SEX.

10 STRATEGIES TO DEAL WITH FEMALE COLLEAGUES IN THE WORKPLACE

1. **Give women an opportunity**, even if they sound, look or think differently. You may be surprised at what they are able to produce.

2. **Not all women are the same**, just as not all men are the same. Despite the brain differences, every person is unique and the time invested to get to know their hopes, fears and motivations will make them feel more engaged and connected.

3. **Do not disregard female intuition.** Women are wired for it and it may be helpful for your business.

4. **Learn to listen to their concerns.** By doing so, you can help them find their own solutions rather than having to do everything yourself.

5. **Connect with your female colleagues** (including junior staff) by asking them on a weekly basis how their projects are going and how they feel about work in general. They will think you are a leader who cares. Be genuine and make eye contact while listening to them.

6. **Have a box of tissues in your office** when you conduct performance appraisals. When a female colleague cries, do not feel obliged to provide a solution. Being present, taking a pause and handing over a tissue may be all you have to do at that point in time.

7. **Ask for feedback about what they think** you need to improve as a leader or fellow worker. You will probably gain good insights if you have developed enough trust with them.

8. **Remember women have hormonal ups and downs**, their moods may fluctuate and their responses may vary throughout the month. This does not make them less effective or less committed to their work.

9. **Offer flexibility.** Women with children need flexibility and are generally very grateful when their manager (or company) allows for it. Do not apply a blanket approach to everybody and respect individual needs.

10. **Ask the women in your team** if you want diversity of thinking and innovative solutions. Do not expect a finished idea, rather take the time to explore and flesh it out as women can provide a variety of alternative options when they are given the time to do so.

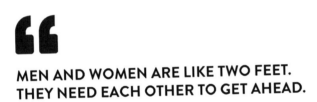

MEN AND WOMEN ARE LIKE TWO FEET. THEY NEED EACH OTHER TO GET AHEAD.

Dr. Helen Fisher

Chapter Four

THE i4 NEUROLEADER MODEL

**LOGIC WILL TAKE YOU FROM A TO B.
IMAGINATION WILL TAKE YOU EVERYWHERE.**

Albert Einstein

SOME OF US MAY HAVE ONCE BEEN TOLD: "IMAGINATION IS FOR CHILDREN. GROW UP AND BEHAVE LIKE AN ADULT!"

WHY DID WE ACCEPT THAT IMAGINATION HAD NO PLACE IN OUR LIVES?

WHY DID WE TRUST THAT BY SETTING UP PROCESSES, RULES AND PROCEDURES, WE WOULD BE SAFE?

BELIEVING THAT A JOB WOULD ALWAYS BE THERE AND WE WOULD LIVE COMFORTABLY EVER AFTER NOW SEEMS LIKE AN ABSTRACT AND UTOPIAN CONCEPT TO ME.

LEADERSHIP FOR THE PRIVILEGED FEW

In the past decades, people in organisations learned to comply with rules, set up performance indicators, wrote manuals about what a manager should or shouldn't do and coached them to have difficult conversations. Yes, I am referring to those one-on-one sessions that make everyone feel apprehensive.

Internal leadership consultants, who may not have led, but possessed the theoretical understanding of what leadership could look like in their organisation, would be hired and spend endless hours creating extensive lists of behaviours for the rest of the management population.

The objective was to get managers to master these behaviours, with limited preparation and training, as the operational work was always seen to be more important. For decades, we thought this was the ideal and we acted accordingly, as if we were hypnotised by some unknown universal force.

We certainly achieved one thing: we made everyone think that 'leadership' is so difficult that most managers believe and still accept that only a few charismatic individuals can ever become great leaders – and based on recent brain scanning of leaders, perhaps they were right. Certain brains are wired in such a way that leadership may be easier for the owners of these brains.

The story in most workplaces ends with the majority of managers being caught up in these processes, repeating the same thing day after day and getting frustrated. Organisations have managed to keep everyone so occupied with the need to complete surplus amounts of paperwork that when it comes to managing people, the time that could have been invested in developing the relationships with team members has simply been erased and consumed by the bureaucracy – just like that.

Or perhaps, the type of leadership that organisations secretly desire has more to do with controlling people rather than inspiring them, so that a certain level of productivity is achieved and the company continues to be financially healthy.

I am inclined to think that this is a more accurate description of the mindsets and beliefs that have prevailed, fostered by the illusion of playing it safe, an illusion that society as a whole has upheld for a long time.

Little did we know that the economic landscape would change forever and that the 'connected' world would bring about a very different workforce, one that suddenly needs to focus on personal leadership. I am not talking about the leadership of Mandela, Winston Churchill or Abraham Lincoln, as these were exceptional leaders, possibly with exceptional brains.

Instead, it is the leadership of becoming the best we can be, of building our self-awareness one day at a time, of learning and growing. The personal leadership that consists of each and every individual discovering who they are and how they can manage all aspects of their lives without waiting for someone else to do it for them.

Currently, people are expected to be able to look after themselves and their careers; and lead a team when required, based on their strengths and skills. Recently, one of my clients described those who could do this as...

"Basically, individuals who dare to think as an exemplary superhero."

The term and the imagery the client created for its corporate high potential program stayed in my mind. After all, superheroes have captured our imaginations for decades. The main message from the stories we read as children was that superheroes used to think more about the common good, rather than about themselves. This would allow them to create a way of behaving that guaranteed they would be beneficial rather than detrimental to the community.

Society has always admired superheroes, probably because we can see in them a set of traits that we would like to own ourselves. Superheroes have the special power to inspire others and the integrity to champion their values, even when everything around them is falling apart. They are confident, inquisitive, conscientious, driven, energetic, adventurous, helpful and generous.

These are the attributes that our new economy requires. We need more superheroes who can collaborate and make a difference, big or small, in their own lives and in the lives of others. The world is becoming a place for makers, not just takers. The world needs people who want to lead and commit to solutions; not people who say "it cannot be done", and adopt compliance as a way of doing business and leading their lives.

As American author and entrepreneur Seth Godin explains in his book "The Icarus Deception" ⊕

CREATING IDEAS THAT SPREAD AND CONNECTING THE DISCONNECTED ARE THE TWO PILLARS OF OUR NEW SOCIETY...

MAINTAINING THE STATUS QUO AND FIGHTING TO FIT IN NO LONGER WORK, BECAUSE OUR ECONOMY AND OUR CULTURE HAVE CHANGED.

Seth Godin

TIMES HAVE CHANGED

These times are very different to what we have always known. We can easily create a video and share it on the internet or blog about an idea we are passionate about and instantly become connected to people we have never met.

These platforms bring empowerment to anyone who is willing to think and act differently. Undoubtedly, this is changing us, taking some by surprise. There are no rules, and chaos is everywhere. A world of possibilities and no certainties.

The most amazing thing is that even though there are no visible rules, or at least none that we can understand, people are still moving forward, creating, taking risks, using this freedom to be themselves and helping others around the globe, just like our beloved superheroes of the past.

As many may find the concept of being a 'superhero' something difficult to replicate, I prefer to use the term "Neuroleader" (as described in Chapter 1).

A Neuroleader is someone who is aware of his/her brain potential (super power) and strives to optimise it. A balanced and functional brain is the foundation for good performance and also the basis of the attributes that characterise the type of leader who could thrive in the "Imagination Age" (as defined by futurologist Rita J. King).

A Neuroleader is a leader with added qualities; someone who can, without a doubt, also do managerial tasks – but would not only be limited to that.

On the next page, there is a table that outlines the differences between a Manager, a Leader and a Neuroleader - as I understand it.

Once again, this is not about leaving some of the traits behind – there will always be overlapping, and the possibility to integrate them based on the situation we are facing.

There will be situations when knowledge may give us the power, but there will be other times when knowledge will be irrelevant because everyone can access it. Under these circumstances, what will differentiate us from the rest is how we then act upon that knowledge.

FROM MANAGER TO NEUROLEADER

The thinking of the person behind the knowledge is what will create value for the economy. People who think similarly will become the loyal followers.

MANAGER *Industrial Age*	LEADER *Information Age*	NEUROLEADER *Imagination Age*
Control = Power	Knowledge = Power	Ideas = Power
Systematic	Visionary	Creator
Task focused	People focused	Brain focused
Measured	Courageous	Vulnerable
I know	We know	Who knows?
No feedback	One-way feedback	Every direction feedback

ON BECOMING A NEUROLEADER

Learning to lead as a Neuroleader may sound a bit intimidating. Below are some strategies to help you become a 'neuroleader':

1. **Become acquainted with your own brain**

   As witty as it may sound, most leaders do not yet think about their brain's functioning at all, naively ignoring the fact that the brain is involved in everything we do.

2. **Aim for self-awareness**

   This is about having the clarity of mind to notice when things become too much to handle and knowing when to ask for help – in case our 'super powers' fail. This type of awareness has to be complemented with the discipline of 'taking a break to recharge', the willingness to accept feedback from others and the ability to adjust our focus.

3. **Minimise paralysis**

   Dealing with the disarray of the unknown that constant change brings is hard, particularly for those who lack confidence and require their viewpoint to be validated before putting the wheels into motion. In corporate jargon, this practice is called dealing with chaos and ambiguity in an agile manner.

4. **Understand the principle of 'human first'**

   Accept that independent of the work we do, we are all human beings with needs, emotions, expectations and desires and that it is perfectly reasonable to show our limitations and say "I do not know". This is a personal journey – a bridge that one has to cross, and this can sometimes be scary.

THE i4 NEUROLEADER MODEL

Leadership models have been developed over time, mainly to help people in organisations focus their attention on what they have to do in order to improve their leadership capabilities.

It is common practice for many organisations to spend money on developing their own internal frameworks to accentuate what is relevant for their leaders to learn.

Some leadership abilities are timeless and will always be expected in those who lead teams, organisations and even their own businesses. Examples of these include: possessing a clear vision; being able to communicate their vision properly; displaying integrity, being commercially astute and business savvy.

As the world changes, the dynamics of leadership have also changed. Most leaders need to think globally and be open to dealing with diverse groups (gender, culture, age, religion). Even when companies act locally, technology has enabled them to reach suppliers who can provide more competitive pricing, thus helping the company to operate with better margins.

Leaders are now able to build partnerships, and their businesses are enlarging and expanding constantly thanks to social media channels and communication tools that connect them instantaneously with people a world away.

The task of leadership, which was previously centred on one individual, is now being shared amongst many. These people are leading simply because they have a particular area of expertise that others don't. These new 'needs' lead to a more aware state of one's own capabilities to satisfy these rapid changes.

In view of everything I have mentioned up to this point, I would like to formally introduce to you the i4 Neuroleader Model, which will be explored in depth over the next few chapters.

THE i4 NEUROLEADER IS A PERSONAL
LEADERSHIP MODEL WITH THE BRAIN
AT ITS CORE.

IT HAS BEEN CREATED FOR THOSE WHO
WISH TO ENHANCE THEIR AWARENESS
AND DEVELOP AS A LEADER.

THIS MODEL INCLUDES FOUR KEY
COMPETENCIES: PERFORMANCE,
COLLABORATION, INNOVATION
AND AGILITY.

INTEGRATION   INSPIRATION   i4   IMAGINATION   INTUITION

PERFORMANCE   COLLABORATION   **i4 NEUROLEADER**   INNOVATION   AGILITY

© SILVIA DAMIANO

TAKING INTO CONSIDERATION
TRADITIONAL LEADERSHIP MODELS
THAT HAVE BEEN USED EXTENSIVELY IN
ORGANISATIONS, THE WORD 'COMPETENCY'
HAS BEEN USED SO PEOPLE CAN EASILY
RELATE TO IT.

IN THE i4 MODEL, 'COMPETENCY'
IS DEFINED AS A COMBINATION
OF OBSERVABLE ABILITIES, TRAITS,
ATTITUDES AND BEHAVIOURS.

THE i4 MODEL EXPANDED

In the i4 Neuroleader Model, each competency is made up of four pillars. The primary pillar for each competency is an 'i' word describing a brain or bodily process: integration, inspiration, imagination and intuition, hence the term 'i4'.

The idea behind this model is to communicate that if leaders want to function better and increase their levels of effectiveness, they need to pay closer attention to how they can tap into these abilities.

PERFORMANCE	COLLABORATION	INNOVATION	AGILITY
● INTEGRATION	● INSPIRATION	● IMAGINATION	● INTUITION
● BALANCE	● COMMUNICATION	● DRIVE	● AWARENESS
● ETHICS	● GENEROSITY	● CURIOSITY	● INFLUENCE
● MENTAL READINESS	● COURAGE	● ATTITUDE	● ADAPTABILITY

© SILVIA DAMIANO

THE UNDERPINNING CONCEPTS

The i4 Neuroleader Model intends to draw attention to three distinctive concepts:

- **A high functioning brain as a leader's best tool:**
  A balanced and healthy brain positively influences a person's behaviour, attention, memory, decision-making and effectiveness. Anyone can get to know his/her brain in more depth and learn how to optimise it.

- **A focus on developing the four 'i' pillars:**
  The pillars of Integration, Inspiration, Imagination and Intuition benefit a person by enhancing his/her capabilities beyond the more habitual brain abilities consisting of analysis, logic and rational thinking; abilities that have been highly valued in the workplace for many decades. These 'i' pillars expand a person's potential, rather than detract from his or her existing abilities.

  ⊙ The 4 i's are shown in the first row of the framework on the left.

- **The most admired attributes in leadership:**
  Arising from countless studies, the timeless attributes that make up the rest of the pillars of the i4 Model are: Balance, Ethics, Mental Readiness, Communication, Generosity, Courage, Drive, Curiosity, Attitude, Awareness, Influence and Adaptability.

  ⊙ The pillars are displayed in the framework on the left.

In no way am I suggesting that the i4 Model needs to be the only framework that is applied in an organisation. However, anyone could easily adopt the i4 Model as the basis to help people develop their 'personal leadership'. Organisations could combine their existing models with the i4 Neuroleader Model.

In a way, this model reflects the ideas and wishes from the many people I have interacted with during workshops, interviews, focus groups and coaching sessions throughout the years.

These individuals have expressed an inner desire to lead better, whilst using abilities that have been ignored and minimised for a long time by their bosses and workplaces.

The abilities of integration, inspiration, imagination and intuition exist within us and, if properly cultivated, can be of great use in business, benefiting the bottom line of any organisation.

PERSONAL LEADERSHIP

Developing personal leadership and becoming a Neuroleader is more associated with how well we use our brains, rather than what job title we have.

With people throughout the world connecting at all levels, personal leadership is becoming more significant than the leadership originating from positional power, which has implications with regards to how we think and act.

What once seemed like a far-away fantasy is today becoming a reality. There are innumerable examples of cross-disciplinary exchanges of knowledge; and due to this, a new understanding of how we could operate as a society is emerging.

Some good examples of these cross-collaborations are the ongoing partnerships between neuroscientists and management professors from different universities and research centres throughout the world. They are working together scanning the brains of leaders and uncovering the secrets of effective leadership.

A recent study led by Professor Sean Hannah from Wake Forest University looked at how the brains of a selected group of leaders work, with the aspiration to create an expert profile.

According to this study – which involved 103 volunteers from the US Military Academy at West Point, ranging in rank from cadet to major – the neural networks of the frontal and prefrontal lobes of those deemed 'leaders' were noticeably different to the rest.

The study concluded that the most successful leaders have more grey matter in places that control decision-making and memory, thus giving them a vital edge when it comes to making the right decisions.

There is no doubt in my mind that these studies, as they are conducted on a more regular basis, will make it easier for us to understand how leaders function and what can be done to enhance brain performance. In my opinion, this has the potential to be applied not only to leaders but to anyone who wants to explore how to expand his or her overall brain function.

The question now is: ➔

HOW LONG WILL IT TAKE FOR ORGANISATIONS TO ACCEPT THESE NEW DISCOVERIES AND CHANGE THE WAY THEY ASSESS AND TRAIN THEIR LEADERS?

NO MONEY FOR LEARNING INITIATIVES

Are You Serious? It saddens me when I hear people working for big, profitable organisations that decide not to allocate any resources towards the development of their leaders.

Recently, a consultant friend of mine joined a very well-known financial institution here in Australia. She is responsible for designing and delivering programs trying to influence the management ranks to lead and communicate more effectively.

She works 13-hour days and with no budget being allocated for leadership development, what she delivers is based simply on her own efforts and existing knowledge.

Needless to say, after two months with the company, she started to feel overly stressed, isolated and abandoned, particularly because managers were not paying any attention to their development, as they chose to devote their attention to the most urgent matters.

Raising the levels of awareness in those who make the decisions and achieving funding are probably the biggest challenges when it comes to supporting leadership initiatives. Another interesting challenge is to find the best brain training tools (there are already some in the market) and influence people to assign the time to use them.

A series of predictions made by SharpBrains (an independent market research firm in the US) estimates that in the near future, more than a million adults in North America alone will take a self-administered annual brain health check up via their iPad or Android tablet. Already in the US, an insurance company is working towards launching an educational campaign to help adults pro-actively take charge of their own 'brain fitness' using digital brain health tools.

Neuroscience is one of the fastest growing areas of interest in contemporary science. It is not only individual brain health and abilities that need to be better understood and utilised at a personal and organisational level, but also for organisations to gain a deeper understanding of how to apply scientific findings when dealing with change and taking better care of their staff and customers. These are only a few of the many areas that this new thinking around Neuroleadership has to offer.

In the following chapters, the i4 model will be explored in depth by outlining what each of the four competencies and the sixteen underpinning pillars mean and their relation to leadership. In conjunction with friend and colleague Tao De Haas, a highly regarded Psychotherapist and executive coach, we have included some ideas to help you further develop, nurture and utilise the four 'i' pillars of integration, inspiration, imagination and intuition.

Chapter Five

THE WAVES OF LEADERSHIP

by Juan Carlos Cubeiro

~

*The following chapter has been written
by my colleague Juan Carlos Cubeiro,
Head of Talent at Manpower Group and
CEO of Right Management in Spain.*

~

LEADERSHIP IS AS OLD AS MANKIND

In fact, at present, leadership makes the difference between organisations that merely survive and those that triumph, between the winning organisations and those that disappear due to a lack of humility.

Throughout history and possibly during prehistory, leadership has been the survival constant because teams (the human groups that obtain synergistic results, achieving more together than individuals in isolation) are winners and there is no team without a leader or leader without a team.

Leadership as a science is relatively recent. It was the 'brainchild' of Californian Warren Gamaliel Bennis more than 50 years ago, who is recognised as the pioneer in the study of leadership. Bennis enrolled at Antioch College in 1947 and Douglas McGregor, one of the founders of modern management theory, was its president.

He took Bennis as his protégé. His ideas made a deep impression on Bennis and today McGregor's "The Human Side of Organisations" remains one of the key texts of management.

In the 1950s, Bennis founded a "Renaissance context" in which modern social science, as we know it now, was born. He collaborated with economists, sociologists, anthropologists and psychologists. Practically all of them were his friends and colleagues and this allowed the "cross-fertilisation" of his ideas.

LEADERSHIP AS A VISION

Bennis' first positioning took place in 1961 with the publication of the article "A Revisionist Theory of Leadership" in which he challenged the conventional wisdom on the subject.

Instead of the 'command and control' myth, of the strong, all-embracing, all-powerful leader, Bennis proposed a closer, more democratic, more participatory leadership style to achieve the proposed objectives. He is considered "the person who transformed leadership into a respectable academic discipline" (Financial Times, 2000).

The 'first wave' of leadership initiated by Bennis is leadership as a future vision. Leaders have to set the pace, which requires them to have self-knowledge, experience and personal ethics because, they must demonstrate the purpose of what they do.

**LEADERSHIP IS THE CAPACITY TO
TRANSLATE THE VISION INTO REALITY.**

Warren Bennis

LEADERSHIP AS A SITUATION

The 'second wave' of leadership begins in the late 1960s with two authors, Ken Blanchard and Paul Hersey, who first published their Situational Leadership model as the "The Life Cycle Theory of Leadership".

The Situational Hersey-Blanchard Theory starts from the premise that leadership style is a function of two variables: the personality of the leader and the maturity of each of the collaborators.

Four types of behaviours determine the leadership style:

- **Telling** (instructions in only one way, because collaborators have little competence and little commitment).

- **Selling** (communication is two-way, but the leader continues to set the direction; although the commitment is greater, the competence is still not adequate).

- **Participating** (collaborators have more experience, analysis and decision-making are shared more).

- **Delegating** (as the competence and commitment of the collaborators grow, they assume the responsibility).

American adult educator Malcolm Knowles is credited with being a fundamental influence in the development of the Humanistic Learning Theory.

He investigated the relationship between these four stages and confirmed that to improve professionally, changes in self-concept, experience, desire to advance and learning orientation are needed.

IN THE PAST, A LEADER WAS A BOSS. TODAY'S LEADERS MUST PARTNER WITH THEIR PEOPLE... THEY CANNOT LEAD BASED ONLY ON THEIR POSITION, ON THEIR POWER.

Ken Blanchard

LEADERSHIP AS TRANSFORMATION

The 'third wave' of leadership came in the 1980s. This was a period of major technological advances and changes (such as Reaganomics, Thatcherism and the fall of the Berlin Wall) and of a greater globalisation.

James McGregor Burns, a historian and political scientist, received the Pulitzer Prize for his work "Roosevelt: The Soldier of Freedom". Burns' focus on leadership is not based on the personality traits of great leaders or on their great deeds, but in the interaction between the leader and his followers. His research is based on how leaders get close to power. Like Bennis, he was a World War II veteran.

Burns contrasts two types of leadership: the transactional, as the name suggests, focuses on the interaction between the leader and his followers while the transformational goes beyond this by focusing on the beliefs, values, interests and needs of the community. This prestigious historian has written that transformational leadership occurs when people are engaged in a project that raises their levels of motivation and morality.

Different experts have followed this perspective of Transformational Leadership, such as Bernard Bass, Bruce Avolio and Kenneth Leithwood.

Bass extended Burns' notion to the psychological mechanisms of the leader and has defined, along with Avolio, the two factors that make this transformation possible:

- The individual consideration of the leader (in terms of empathy, trust and honest communication). Transformational leaders challenge members of their teams to be more creative and innovative, to not settle for the status quo and to bring new ideas and change.

- The inspiration (from an exciting vision that promotes collaborators to give the best of themselves) and idealised influence (where the leader is an example, a role model to their followers).

LEADERSHIP AS EMOTION

In 1990, Peter Salovey of Yale University and John Mayer, from the University of New Hampshire, developed the concept of 'Emotional Intelligence' creating the 'fourth' wave of leadership. They wondered whether the combination of both terms was pure contradiction.

However, American developmental psychologist Howard Gardner had already established the "multiple intelligences" (up to eight), two of which are intra-personal intelligence and interpersonal intelligence. Salovey and Mayer define emotional intelligence as ⊕

"The ability to manage one's own emotions and those of others, to discriminate among them and to use this information to guide one's thoughts and actions."

They thought of emotional intelligence as something that could be split into three areas:

- The evaluation and expression,

- the regulation,

- and the use of emotion.

Daniel Jay Goleman, Doctor in Psychology from Harvard University and journalist for the science pages of The New York Times for 12 years, published "Emotional Intelligence: Why it Can Matter more than IQ" in 1995. Goleman's book was a major hit (more than a year and a half on the best-seller list of The New York Times), with more than 5 million copies sold. Daniel Goleman imagined that it would transform the world of education, but where it awakened major interest was in management.

Between 1998 and 2013, he published many articles in the *Harvard Business Review* magazine and wrote many books on leadership, emotional and social intelligence.

Leadership is more than 90% pure emotional intelligence – our ability to manage one's own emotions and the emotions of others.

In his books, Goleman speaks of four domains:

- Self-awareness (skills related to self-knowledge and self-confidence)

- Self-regulation (self-control skills and results orientation)

- Empathy (orientation to others, altruism)

- Social capacity (teamwork, honest influence)

In 2001, in his book "Primal Intelligence", Goleman and co-authors Richard Boyatzis and Annie McKee connected emotional intelligence with leadership through six styles:

- Imposing

- Exemplary

- Cohesive

- Participatory

- Guiding

- Trainer

Goleman's most recent work is "Focus: The Hidden Driver of Excellence." This is a very innovative view of the scarce and possibly most underrated talent in modern society: attention. Goleman has found that professionals in business, the arts or sports stand out dramatically when they cultivate visualisation, focus or practise meditation. It is a matter of focusing properly.

Attention is a subtle power that requires comprehension, memory and learning. It is a little known and recognised ability that American neuroscientists Michael Posner and Mary Rothbart defined as ⊕

"The mechanism that underlies our consciousness and voluntary control of our thoughts and feelings."

THE EMOTIONAL BRAIN RESPONDS FASTER TO AN EVENT THAN THE RATIONAL BRAIN.

Daniel Goleman

LEADERSHIP AS TRAINING

The 'fifth wave' of leadership is about talent development (our own and that of our collaborators), with the notion of a leader also being a coach.

The initiator or this wave was Jack Zenger, best-selling author and consultant with more than five decades of experience in leadership development who has taught at Stanford University since 1994 and is a world-renowned expert in human resources.

He has written "The Extraordinary Leader", "The Inspiring Leader" and "The Extraordinary Coach." To Zenger, great leaders work on their strengths and not on their weaknesses and this is precisely what makes them extraordinary.

In addition, the best leaders build trust and cooperation in their teams to get especially good results. Extraordinary leaders excel in the skill to "inspire and motivate to achieve high performance." Thus, the climate of the team will be one of confidence, optimism, hope, initiative, responsibility and resilience.

Zenger and co-author Kathleen Stinett based their work on the research by Dr. James Prochaska, a psychologist who has worked with people who want to overcome their addictions. His "theory of change" shows step by step how people can be transformed from low performance to high performance. It is about learning at a faster rate than the environment to be able to survive. Therefore, leadership as training (and as coaching) is very valuable.

WHILE ALL EMOTIONS ARE CONTAGIOUS, A LEADER'S BEHAVIOUR UNLEASHES AN EPIDEMIC FOR BETTER OR FOR WORSE.

Jack Zenger

LEADERSHIP AS A SOLUTION TO THE COMPLEXITY OF OUR TIMES

To better understand how leadership has evolved through the contributions of experts, we can use the metaphor of the captain of a ship.

The captain needs to steer the ship towards the port he wants to go (Visionary Leadership); to adapt what he does based on the type of ship and crew he has (Situational Leadership); to do things better and in a different way (Transformational Leadership); he/she needs the emotions of the crew to be positive (Emotional Leadership), and it is also required that the captain develops their talent (Trainer Leadership).

Now the question is: how would the ship face a 'perfect storm', a set of circumstances that would make the journey particularly complex and difficult?

We live in a 'VUCA World' (Volatility, Uncertainty, Complexity and Ambiguity), an acronym derived from military terminology. This term also applies to strategy and leadership. It is a volatile world because it changes dynamics more frequently than ever. It is uncertain because of its unpredictability. It is complex because many variables are involved at once and ambiguous because cause and effect sequences do not work as they previously did and reality seems to be the result of randomness.

This new VUCA era caused the US Army to review its leadership manual and transform it into the 'Be-Know-Do' model, relying more than ever on competence, character and action-taking.

Who makes a difference in a VUCA world? 'Anti-fragile' leaders, according to author Nassim Nicholas Taleb, a Lebanese American essayist, scholar and statistician. Taleb believes that both society as a whole, and specifically the economy, are more fragile than ever due to overprotection. The answer to this problem is anti-fragile leadership, a leadership that is more resilient and robust. A style that is able to grow from challenges and become stronger.

In a VUCA world, according to Duke University's Professor Rick Voirin, the strategic dilemmas are irresolvable, complex, threatening, enigmatic, confusing and multiple. Therefore, the key skills needed for leadership in this VUCA era include: the ability to learn from the strangest situations; to see things from the point of view of nature; to calm down and integrate opposing positions; to be open and authentic in what is important and to create and innovate constantly.

The answer to a VUCA World is precisely what leadership expert Silvia Damiano offers through her i4 Neuroleader Model:

- **Integration**
  A high performing and balanced brain that is able to realise the connections between the different variables of this very 'Complex' world.

- **Inspiration**
  To overcome the 'Uncertainty' generated by such unpredictability.

- **Imagination**
  To deal with the dynamics of change, which make the conditions very 'Volatile'.

- **Intuition**
  To resolve the 'Ambiguity' of our times, in which the sequences of simple and linear 'cause and effect' no longer work.

The i4 Model incorporates the latest advances from neuroscience and neuroleadership — the practical application of brain science to the leadership domain.

Silvia Damiano provides a distinctive approach to what leadership needs to look like in our times: **Leadership as a solution to the complexity.**

In contrast to the previous leadership models, which mainly originated in Anglo-Saxon countries, the i4 Model is the product of someone who was raised in Latin America and has lived and worked in several continents. Silvia's global experience has allowed her to develop a holistic view in regards to leadership.

Furthermore, the i4 Model takes into account the abilities that the female gender is more inclined to adopt when leading. This brings to mind the research by Dr. Louanne Brizendine on how women's right and left hemispheres of the brain are more interconnected in comparison to men's. This difference results in women being able to communicate more openly, an important quality in leadership.

Additionally, women are able to detect facial expressions 90% of the time, while men are only able to capture the subtle signs of emotions 40% of the time. This gives the female gender the capacity to be more empathetic towards others.

Another significant difference is the hormone testosterone, which is higher in men. This makes men demonstrate a more commanding and goal-focused approach when leading others.

Does a different brain mean different leadership? It is very possible.

Section Two

EXPLORING THE
i4 MODEL COMPETENCIES

~

This section delves deeper into the neuroscience behind the i4 Neuroleader Model.

Explore the sixteen pillars and learn how to apply these concepts within the leadership realm.

~

Chapter Six

THE COMPETENCIES & PILLARS IN DETAIL

THE i4 PILLARS

By now, you would have become acquainted with the i4 Model and come to terms with how important it is to develop a more holistic view of people's capabilities, both your own and those of others.

Due to the amount of research that is continuously appearing in relation to the brain and leadership behaviours, it is impossible not to weave some of this new knowledge into the i4 Neuroleader Model when explaining each of the pillars.

In this chapter, I describe the elements that make up each pillar and in the chapters that follow, I have devoted an entire section to explain the four 'i' pillars (integration, inspiration, imagination and intuition) in more depth.

My reasons for doing this are:

- The 'i' pillars are the abilities that we can all develop without too much effort.

- It is cost effective.

- It maximises human performance and improves engagement.

- It increases profit.

- It provides the sense of empowerment that most people desire.

As we stand on the brink of a change of era, it is regrettable to think that these fundamental human abilities have basically been ignored in terms of leadership and management practices. But for those who are observant and forward thinkers, it is not that difficult to see that when these abilities are encouraged, they can ignite passion within those who learn and use them.

Within the context of organisations, the leaders who attract and retain the best talent will be the ones who are willing to value and promote the significance of using the brain effectively, who allocate time for their employees to explore their creativity and who have the courage to dismantle heavy and bureaucratic structures in order to invite participation and decision-making.

Being aware of the existence of these 'i' abilities and keeping them in mind will absolutely change the way you work when it comes to managing both your own and others' performance, collective intelligence, innovation and adaptive capabilities.

Developing the 4 'i' abilities entails:

- ○ Keeping your brain and body in the best possible condition (integration).

- ○ Being willing to turn negative emotions into more positive ones to enhance your zest for life for yourself and others (inspiration).

- ○ Assigning the time to activate the brain circuits that foster creative moments (imagination).

- ○ Giving yourself permission to recognise and use your intuitive insights without feeling odd about it (intuition).

For the chapters on inspiration, imagination and intuition, I decided to work alongside psychotherapist, executive coach and my good friend – Tao de Haas.

Tao is a living example of how to live a life using these specific abilities. Having relied heavily on them himself when navigating his school years with dyslexia, he is a firm believer in applying them to his daily professional practice.

Please note:
When reading the descriptions in this chapter, keep in mind that using one word to express the myriad of behaviours, abilities, attitudes and traits may not represent the understanding of everyone. One word may be interpreted differently depending on a person's background and the context in which it is used.

If you find yourself thinking that perhaps a more appropriate word could have been used in reference to the elements that I will be describing, please know that you may be correct, as it has proven quite a tricky task to make such selections.

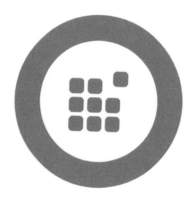

PERFORMANCE

Performance refers to the optimal level, both mental and physical, that a person is able to achieve when implementing a task.

Achieving optimal performance depends on how well your brain-mind-body system is functioning; the time and dedication you devote to mentally prepare for a task (particularly when it is challenging); how you regulate and balance your daily activities, and how congruent and aligned you are in terms of your values and moral reasoning.

WHAT TO LOOK FOR IN A PERSON →

HIGH PERFORMANCE

- Generally feels at ease and happy about life
- Takes care of his/her body, mind & spirit
- Is confident without being arrogant
- Is good at managing both tasks and relationships
- Knows both the potential and limitations of his/her brain
- Can remain calm in stressful situations
- Has good judgment and common sense
- Is focused, disciplined and knows how to prioritise
- Usually makes good decisions

LOW PERFORMANCE

- Lacks self-awareness
- Loses control of his/her emotions easily
- Has not developed good social and communication skills
- Does not know how to plan ahead
- Often makes the wrong decisions
- Procrastinates
- Usually becomes defensive when interacting with others
- Is inconsistent between his/her words and actions
- Is easily overwhelmed by situations and people
- Does not know how to balance life activities

*When our brains function well,
we have the power to tell stories
and the intelligence to discern which
stories are to be believed.*

~

Silvia Damiano

THE PILLARS OF PERFORMANCE ➔

Performing optimally both at work and in life requires certain basic abilities, but above all, it requires 'maintenance'.

Nobody would even consider driving a long way without making a series of stops throughout the journey to refuel the car. However, in today's fast-paced world, for one reason or another, many people work frantically and develop bad habits which make them less effective, without even being conscious of it.

Our brains and bodies form a system and failing to take care of this system may lead to mood disorders, poor performance and disease (mental, physical or emotional).

The pillars of Performance are: Integration, Balance, Ethics and Mental Readiness.

In the sections that follow, you will learn what these four pillars refer to within the context of the i4 Model.

INTEGRATION

Integration refers to the effective functioning of the various components of the brain and body that result in a healthy system.

An integrated system may be evident in a person who is mostly calm but also alert, mindful, energised and pleasant to deal with.

EXECUTIVE FUNCTION

The area of the brain just behind the forehead is called the Prefrontal Cortex (PFC).

This area is known as the 'orchestrator' of everything we do and is the seat of consciousness. The PFC is involved in decision-making, planning, abstract reasoning, judgment, short-term memory, impulse-control and is responsible for sustaining attention and inhibiting distractions.

In relation to leadership

Leadership is not a simple task. To a certain extent, it relies on how well the PFC operates and how a leader can demonstrate the capacities mentioned above. When the PFC works well, people are alert, as well as calm, towards themselves and others. They can focus, establish goals and be conscious of what they say and the impact they have on others. Followers relate better to 'conscious' leaders.

MIND-BODY ALIGNMENT

The most important qualities of a human being can be expressed when an individual personally transforms and is able to offer a broader gamut for effective thinking and action.

Stressful environments prevent people from achieving this and can lead to a disconnection between what they truly feel (sensations in their bodies), what they think (in their minds) and how they actually behave or act in front of others.

In relation to leadership

Leaders who are able to perceive their emotions (the first step towards building mind-body alignment) and realise how to bring the three brains (gut, heart and head brain) into line can indeed strengthen their self-awareness, adjust more efficiently to life's stressors and manage their responses in a way that builds others' confidence instead of weakens it.

THE 'CARE' FACTOR

Recent neuro-imaging studies reveal that performing analytical tasks uses different brain networks to those responsible for social skills (i.e. caring).

While one network goes quiet, the other is active. Since the brain naturally operates in this way, leaders may need to better balance the time spent on people as opposed to the time spent focusing on achieving results. It is also critical to minimise stress, as this can overload the social circuits and affect how much attention we are willing or capable of giving to others.

In relation to leadership

One of the attributes that best correlates with leadership effectiveness is the ability to care about others. It is well documented that the No. 1 reason why people leave organisations is because of issues with their direct manager.

A leader who knows how to connect and show empathy and compassion towards others is without any doubt more respected and admired.

Your brain is the organ of your personality, character, and intelligence and is heavily involved in making you who you are.

~

Daniel G. Amen

BALANCE

Balance refers to a series of actions and attitudes that may help a person keep the brain performing at its best.

Latest research findings suggest that the brain and body's homoeostatic (balanced) state is better managed when individuals assign the time and attention to a series of actions that can assist them in dealing with tough situations without affecting their performance and well-being. There are three aspects that help to define the pillar of balance:

PHYSICALITY

Committing to a good nutritional plan, exercising and allocating time for relaxation and play are fundamental steps towards good health and productivity.

Physical activity can also enhance resilience through a number of neurobiological mechanisms by boosting endorphins and neurotransmitters, such as dopamine and serotonin, which reduce the risk of depression. Exercise also suppresses the release of the stress hormone cortisol.

In relation to leadership

Setting an example is an important leadership quality. When leaders lack good physical health or are in a continuous state of tension, they can create hectic environments and role model undesirable behaviours. A body that is healthy helps the brain to be sharper, providing the person with the internal strength to face the difficulties that may arise while taking an organisation from A to B successfully.

DOWN TIME

What people do in their down time really matters when it comes to brain functioning.

Time spent 'doing nothing' or simply being in the moment, as well as getting the proper amount of sleep, are two brain activities which have been increasingly ignored by many. They can affect people's capacity to decide, concentrate, be creative or have a positive mood.

On average, people sleep one hour less per night than they did twenty years ago, and in most workplaces, people run from one meeting to the next without giving the brain an opportunity to compose itself.

In relation to leadership

When people are well rested and take regular breaks, their memories improve, they retain information better, they have more clarity of thinking, can assess complex situations, make better judgments and are more inclined to consider others' points of view. In a world which demands that we use our cognitive capacities more than ever, the consequences of not balancing our active time with down time is an issue to be discussed and reviewed.

SOCIABILITY

The brain is wired to be social and when we feel rejected or isolated, it is affected in the same way as when we feel physical pain.

Keeping the brain circuits active by socialising with others is crucial for human beings, as a lack of interactions (water cooler conversations, open discussions about ideas, social gatherings to simply talk about life) can lead people into an isolated state. This reinforces the mindset that focusing on the task and achieving deadlines are the only things that seem to matter the most.

In relation to leadership

At Google, a program to foster empathy and sociability was developed and successfully run for a number of years. Its purpose was to train highly analytical and technical people (and leaders) in the importance of connecting with others, with the aim of promoting cross-pollination of ideas and a sense of connection, which are both exceptionally important in making a business successful.

*If a brain is exercised properly,
anyone can grow intelligence,
at any age, and potentially by a lot.
Or you can just let your brain idle
- and watch it slowly, inexorably,
go to seed like a sedentary body.*

~

Dr. Michael Merzenich

ETHICS

Ethics refers to the set of moral values and principles that guide a person's actions and enable him/her to differentiate between right and wrong.

The act of reflecting and finding congruence among one's own values, emotions, thoughts and actions has a direct impact on people's display of their ethical standards and consequently their leadership effectiveness. There are three aspects that help to define the pillar of ethics:

VALUES

Values determine what is important for a person; hence, they help guide what actions and decisions he/she may take.

Analysing values and motivators has always been a topic of interest to psychologists and philosophers. At a symposium organised by the Foundation IPSEN in Paris, in 2005, a new perspective on human values based on neurobiology was introduced. The things that reward the brain or what the brain may get addicted to can affect, to some extent, whether people stick to their values or not.

In relation to leadership

In the 2005 documentary film "Enron: The Smartest Guys in the Room", which tells the story of the collapse of the American energy corporation, a scene depicts real interviews with the traders who used to work for the company. One of the highlights from these interviews is their acknowledgement of how they ignored their most basic values in the pursuit of financial returns.

Driven by greed, their brains tricked them into thinking that what they may have held as important was no longer the case and that any means justified the final goal.

To unravel why this may happen, neuroscientific studies have delved into the effect of greed on the brain and have found that greed has a similar effect to drugs such as cocaine on the brain's reward circuits.

JUDGMENT

Judgment is the ability to perceive, understand, evaluate and make considered decisions.

It is known that poor judgment is associated with suboptimal functioning of the prefrontal cortex (PFC). A new field of research called 'decision neuroscience' is focused on trying to determine what specific neuronal circuits in the brain are involved with decisions and mapping thinking on a cellular level.

In relation to leadership

Research on judgment has attracted a lot of attention from the scientific community as each and every one of us has to make countless decisions on a daily basis. In businesses, the capacity to judge and make suitable decisions is one of the most highly sought after leadership capabilities.

Even though we would like to think that leaders make great decisions, the reality is that on many occasions they are flawed, and unfortunately the consequences of these decisions are only seen long after they have taken place. Researchers agree that flawed decisions usually start with errors of judgment made by influential individuals.

CONGRUENCY

Congruency implies a person saying what they really mean and living (or practising) what they believe in by showing consistency in every aspect of who they are (body language, tone of voice, facial expressions, attitudes and actions).

In relation to leadership

Congruency determines how reliable the leader is, as perceived by others. When leaders are able to genuinely display the behaviours they want to see happening in their organisations and stand by their principles, the outcome is more likely to be achieved. Congruent leaders are usually more interested in empowering others, rather than in enhancing their own status or prestige.

*A quiet conscience makes
one strong.*

~

Anne Frank

MENTAL READINESS

Mental readiness refers to the ability of a person to create a balanced psychological state in which he or she can perform at an optimal level.

A person who is mentally ready has mastered the capacity to focus, self-manage and maintain a healthy degree of internal discipline, which provides him or her with the confidence and ability to fully enjoy the challenge or task ahead. The three aspects below help to define the pillar of mental readiness:

CONFIDENCE

For Olympic athletes, their internal state of confidence in regards to their capacities, potential, purpose, preparation and the people who support them is what can convert them into champions.

In an initial study led by Dr. Benedetto De Martino from the Royal Holloway University of London, with the purpose of identifying the parts of the brain associated with confidence, two regions (the ventromedial and the right rostrolateral prefrontal cortex) were found to be active along with variations of subjective confidence.

In relation to leadership

In business, as opposed to the world of sports, people value and encourage confidence in themselves and others in a very casual, often random manner, possibly as a consequence of tight organisational structures and bosses who ignore the fact that healthy levels of confidence are related to the achievement of a goal or vision.

Confidence, however, is a key determinant of the decisions we make and how we work and relate to others. More often than not, it comes from our awareness.

FOCUS

The capacity to focus or refocus is the most important mental skill associated with being ready to perform.

Despite its significance, being 'distracted' has become more frequent, even a malady. In a world dominated by information overload and recurrent interruptions from technological devices, as well as 'open-space' offices designed with the illusion that they are the best thing that has ever happened, distractions have become the 'new enemy'. Perhaps, in time, our brains will rewire themselves and adapt to this constant multi-sensorial input without causing any stress; however, this is yet to be seen.

For now, people's capacity to pay full attention to another individual or to a task and inhibit other distractions depends entirely on their power to concentrate — a skill which is intimately connected to the degree of development and functioning of the prefrontal cortex, the great protagonist of our lives (particularly of our working lives).

In relation to leadership

It is not unusual to see people on the street completely oblivious to what is happening in their surroundings while obsessively looking at their mobile phone; or to see co-workers sit in workplace meetings with absent-minded looks on their faces. In both cases, the lack of present-moment focus can affect their cognitive capacities.

The ability to focus can provide a leader with a greater ability to recall information, a more stable mood and increased levels of performance. It is not surprising that the practice of mindfulness has become the easiest and most highly regarded tool to address the lack of mental focus.

PLANNING

In emergency services and in the military, the activities undertaken by any team are usually planned in advance before the action starts, as a lack of planning can result in a loss of lives or injuries (physical, mental or emotional).

Usual planning activities may consist of:

- Visualising the situation and its probable outcomes before it happens

- Drawing out a plan of action that aligns to the goal or goals

- Preparing physically (breathing and centering)

- Positively reinforcing people's thoughts through words or marching songs (like they do in the army)

- Breaking the mission into pieces (chunking it down), particularly when it is dangerous (i.e. putting out a bush fire or patrolling unsafe streets).

Proper planning can help the executive part of the brain to think more clearly and be prepared to deal with the unknown, without feeling threatened or weighed down.

In relation to leadership

Those who fail to plan, fail to perform. Taking time to plan before a meeting, a presentation or a difficult conversation requires a certain level of mapping out a strategy to achieve excellent execution. Planning in business could involve things such as: writing what needs to be communicated, mentally rehearsing the conversation or speech, imagining possible questions or objections, knowing how to address an audience and speaking positively to oneself, particularly if the situation is a challenging one.

*By failing to prepare,
you are preparing to fail.*

~

Benjamin Franklin

COLLABORATION

Collaboration refers to the attainment of a common goal through the effort of a combined body of people working together.

True collaboration starts with one's own desire to share and inspire others towards the achievement of an ideal that can turn into a concrete outcome. Communicating openly and having the courage to overcome conflict are as important as being generous with knowledge, resources and time.

WHAT TO LOOK FOR IN A PERSON

HIGH COLLABORATION

- Is tolerant and accepting of others' views and perspectives
- Can say please, sorry and thank you without feeling troubled
- Aims to achieve rather than compete
- Believes that a good team accomplishes more than just an individual
- Knows how to engage others
- Speaks with conviction and passion
- Likes to teach or coach others
- Is both caring and courageous
- Knows when and how to praise others
- Listens, asks meaningful questions and articulates his/her inner thoughts and feelings with clarity

LOW COLLABORATION

- Is self-centred
- Is reluctant to provide help to others
- Is usually thinking what he/she can gain from a situation
- Is fearful of losing
- Likes to work in isolation
- Is competitive
- May have a sense of superiority
- Has trouble delegating tasks
- Can be rude, harsh or disrespectful towards others
- Does not know how to deal with conflict

Individually, we are one drop.
Together, we are an ocean.

~

Ryunosuke Satoro

THE PILLARS OF COLLABORATION

Due to technological advances over the last two decades, collaboration has become one of the most highly valued competencies of the modern workplace.

The emergence of virtual teams and a global economy requires employees and businesses to have the ability to work fluidly across boundaries, understand how diversely people think, and lead functional teams that can accomplish their goals successfully.

The pillars of Collaboration are: Inspiration, Communication, Generosity and Courage.

In the sections that follow, you will learn what these 4 pillars refer to within the context of the i4 Model.

INSPIRATION

Inspiration refers to the energy, enthusiasm and desire to act, as a result of feeling mentally and emotionally stimulated.

Being able to inspire and motivate oneself translates into inspiring and enthusing others. People are more likely to share and encourage others to work with them when inspiration is the underlying motivation. There are three aspects that help to define the pillar of inspiration:

VISION

Vision is the ability of one's mind to clearly see a specific and/or desired outcome at some point in the future.

A person who has a vision may not necessarily have worked out the strategy or steps needed to get there; but the capacity to develop the vision is a vital factor towards being inspired and in turn, inspiring others. It provides us with impetus, a sense of "want", and a dream to pursue. It is linked to a person's ability to imagine and mentally create a picture of something that has not yet been created or achieved.

In relation to leadership

Visionary leaders strongly believe that what they are able to imagine can turn into reality. They are generally optimistic in the pursuit of their vision and are able to communicate what the vision is about to attract others to it. Anyone can expand their visionary abilities by stepping back from their operational tasks and learning to reflect on 'what could be', rather than on 'what is'. Doing this creates new connections in the brain and triggers novel thoughts in relation to future potential.

PASSION

Passion is a strong emotion that moves people to do their best. Without it, major advancements in every aspect of society would have never taken place.

Passion makes people feel inspired and excited. It is the emotional energy that drives humans to invent, discover and carry out projects and other endeavours. Researchers believe passion is linked to the neurotransmitter dopamine – a chemical that is released in the brain when we anticipate receiving some kind of reward from what we are about to do. Also referred to as the 'chemical of desire', this substance is involved with both attention and motivation. Low levels of dopamine are associated with depression, a tendency to acquire addictions and a lack of drive.

In relation to leadership

John Hagel, Co-Chairman of the Deloitte Center of Innovation in San Francisco, remarkably links passion to performance in business, stating in one of his great blog posts that "people pursuing their passion are deeply committed to the domain that has engaged them."

According to Hagel, passionate people "have both a deep sense of integrity about their quest and demanding expectations about themselves in terms of performance." For these people, it is not about achieving their full potential; it is about their potential being constantly expanded by new possibilities."

TRUST

If there is one thing that defines human relationships (both personally and professionally), it is the ability to trust.

When a sense of confidence from one person to another grows, relationships flourish and outcomes are more likely to be achieved. Recent scientific research reveals that trust is correlated with the hormone oxytocin, which promotes bonding in humans and also assists in breaking down social barriers, thus increasing a sense of trust, self-esteem and optimism.

In relation to leadership

In a new economy where collaboration has started to reign, power-based relationships are being reshaped into those based on trusting others and knowing how to be trusted. The continuous push and consequent compulsion of some leaders to spend most of their working hours on action-related tasks has detracted from the time that needs to be devoted to building up trust within their teams.

Trust is critical in dealing with conflict constructively, when communicating and when discussing goals in a motivating, rather than a commanding manner.

*You see things and you say "Why?"
But I dream things that never were;
and I say "Why not?".*

~

George Bernard Shaw

COMMUNICATION

Communication is a well-developed set of abilities to impart information or exchange thoughts, ideas and feelings with others.

A clear articulation of what is needed and the ability to actively listen to the wishes of other people are the foundational steps for connecting and engaging with others. There are three aspects that help to define the pillar of communication:

PRESENCE

The expression "I see you", which is also the theme song of the movie Avatar, derives from a greeting customary to South African tribes.

This salutation reminds people of the importance of being present for anyone they greet. However, as useful, enjoyable and respectful this practice is to set the tone of how we communicate with one another, the current reality is that humans have learnt to rush and get distracted when interacting with others, instead of being present. The ability to be in the moment not only facilitates feelings of acknowledgement and appreciation towards others, but also builds common understanding and alignment.

In relation to leadership

Leaders who are able to manage their emotions of impatience and defensiveness and listen attentively by stopping their inner monologue in the presence of others, are better positioned to establish the type of connections that most people aspire to have. Two well-known examples of total presence are the Dalai Lama and former US President Bill Clinton. Those who have been in contact with either of them have stated feeling 'in awe' at their level of presence and the attention that they confer to every person they come in contact with, even for a few moments.

SELF-EXPRESSION

Having the ability to articulate one's inner thoughts, ideas and needs in a clear, concise and convincing manner is something to be learnt and mastered.

Quite often, people are certain that they have expressed their perspectives or requirements and that others will act upon them, only to find out later that the message has not been fully understood and no action has been taken. Knowing how to say what needs to be said in a way that matches the audience's style of gathering information, as well as learning to check if the message was understood, is crucial for anyone who wants to maximise communication flow.

In relation to leadership

It is useful for people who aspire to lead teams and organisations to be cognisant of how they convey their messages if they are to do well in their communication efforts. Over and over, people are afraid of speaking up and seem unable to find the right words to address the issue in a precise and graceful manner. This can generate a void that amplifies tension that may already exist, thus creating more doubts and misunderstanding among those who are on the receiving end.

CHUNKING DOWN

*Working in an increasingly complex world requires considering multiple aspects
of a situation and inferring possible solutions without having all the evidence.*

While some people seem to have a strategic eye and the ability to think 'complexly',
others struggle with it. One of the processes frequently used in the field of Neuro-Linguistic
Programming is called 'chunking down'. This process is used to understand abstract concepts
and easily communicate to others what to do when having to deal with a complex or difficult
problem. To 'chunk down' means to break up the big picture, which may sometimes
be overwhelming, into manageable pieces (or chunks) that are more concrete and specific.

In relation to leadership

While some personality types enjoy the abstract, the unknown and the complex, others seek
practical and concrete steps to follow, but there is a continuum between these two extremes.
A leader who pushes everyone to deal with complexity needs to understand that this range
exists and the more clarity and certainty that is provided to people, the better the understanding
will be.

Complexity means that we have to deal with things that are unpredictable and that there
is no guarantee of what may happen next. Considering that some people's brains look for
certainty and the lack of it can cause distress, leaders who take this into account can minimise
stressful moments.

*The single biggest problem
in communication is the illusion
that it has taken place.*

~

George Bernard Shaw

GENEROSITY

Generosity refers to the kind disposition and altruistic manner that a person displays when dealing and interacting with others.

When people learn to think beyond themselves and are able to develop a generous approach towards those around them, a sense of collective energy is generated. This translates into the willingness to contribute to the 'cause', whatever this might be. There are three aspects that help to define the pillar of generosity:

A WIN-WIN APPROACH

Opting for a win-win approach as a way of working collaboratively with others taps into the deep-seated sense of fairness that many uphold as an important value.

Competitiveness, on the other hand, requires that someone wins while someone else loses. This mainly applies to sports and sometimes it can be unavoidable in certain business deals. However, a win-win strategy can solve conflict more effectively and build long-lasting relationships with members of any group. The nature of working relationships that is starting to prevail in the marketplace (micropreneurs, independent consultants, out-sourced partners) functions more smoothly with the mindset that everyone can win, rather than "I win and you lose."

In relation to leadership

Leaders who focus primarily on winning while ignoring the needs and ideas that others can provide may soon feel out of place as 'competitors'. In a society that is rapidly embracing a more collaborative approach to work, this is a poor strategy to pursue. When leaders are able to work on being open and flexible in adopting new ideas (particularly those of others), they are more likely to develop a win-win mindset.

THINKING BEYOND SELF

In nature, many animals survive by staying together and helping one another. Showing solidarity, even between different species, is not unusual.

Such is the case of zebras and antelopes in Africa, which warn each other when a predator approaches. In the past few decades, the capacity to think beyond oneself has diminished as people have become busier and more stressed. Under these conditions, displaying our natural gestures of solidarity and heroism seem to only appear in moments of tragedy or catastrophe.

In relation to leadership

The assumption that success mostly depends on individual effort and that selfishness, greed and competition are the key drivers to achieve the desired financial results has proven to be quite a fallacy in recent times. The Global Financial Crisis (GFC) and its consequences for the world economy have been driven predominantly by the egotistical behaviours of 'leaders' and their underdeveloped capacity for solidarity or cooperation and their lack of awareness of how their actions affect others.

WILLINGNESS TO HELP

Doing good things for others not only warms the heart, but also protects it.

People who help or volunteer on a regular basis are more likely to use and strengthen their empathetic and altruistic behaviours, as well as improving their own motivation and physical health (better heart functioning and lower cholesterol levels).

In relation to leadership

Anyone in a position of leadership has the opportunity to help others by coaching them, teaching, mentoring or simply actively listening to their concerns. Generally, people will value the time and support that a leader can provide when it comes to guiding them in their careers and they are more likely to stay around if they feel engaged and connected with their teams and organisations.

Generosity is giving more than you can, and pride is taking less than you need.

~

Kahlil Gibran

COURAGE

Courage refers to the ability of a person to face difficult circumstances despite being fearful.

This includes the fortitude to say what needs to be said, in an appropriate and timely manner and the wisdom to know when to accept what cannot be changed. There are three aspects that help to define the pillar of courage:

FEAR MANAGEMENT

In the middle of the brain (limbic system), two small structures called amygdala, one in each hemisphere of the brain, are believed to be responsible for controlling our fear responses.

However, new research indicates that the response to fear also involves other regions besides the amygdala (brain-stem, insular cortex). Disentangling the mechanisms of fear and how to manage any excessive amygdala activation and the consequent emotional reactions has become an important subject of scientific studies. Understanding these mechanisms could certainly make people's interactions in any context more stable rather than reactionary, therefore minimising conflict.

In relation to leadership

Although our brains seem to have the primary function of helping us survive by detecting threats in our environments, these primordial reactions are sometimes out of context in our current working environments, where people's defensiveness damages relationships. The SCARF model – which consists of five domains: Status, Certainty, Autonomy, Relatedness and Fairness – provides an easy-to-grasp framework that can help leaders understand what may drive certain fear-based reactions in people, when their inner needs are not being met by others.

This concept, developed by Dr. David Rock, is based on the theory that these five social drivers activate the primary reward or threat circuitry in the brain. This circuitry is similar to the brain networks that become active when one's life is in danger. Understanding this model may enable leaders to design interactions with others in a way that minimises the threat response.

ABILITY TO REDIRECT EFFORTS

When things don't go according to plan, looking at the bigger picture, working out a feasible solution and redirecting efforts while letting go of self-doubt depends on an inner ability called 'self-efficacy' – a term coined in 1997 by American psychologist Albert Bandura.

Having the fortitude to find the way amongst opposing conditions and the deep belief that, no matter how, the results can still be achieved, is a great capability to instil in ourselves and in those who work with us.

In relation to leadership

Managers who use fear-based strategies, secrecy and punishment methods to maintain control, limit the potential of their businesses and create disengagement. Relying on threats to get something done belongs to an old way of leading others.

On the other hand, believing in the people that work for you, accepting failure as a necessary step towards success and redirecting efforts when things are not working while providing frequent feedback, are possibly the most suitable strategies to lead in this new era of work.

TRYING NEW THINGS

It is quite common to see people stuck in the past, repeating patterns of behaviour and duplicating what they have learnt from others in situations that may be entirely different from what is actually occurring.

It requires a certain level of willingness and courage to stop this rumination process (dwelling on past issues and concerns in our heads), to let go of what we experienced in the past and dare to try new things without constraints.

The ability to forget past thoughts and deal with the present more effectively may depend on how well we are able to suppress certain memories. Neuroscientists are now studying these inhibitory processes in the brain as a way for people to stop bringing unnecessary memories into the present that can limit their ability to try new things.

In relation to leadership

Knowing your team members in depth by asking about their life experiences, values, needs and desires is a way to understand how they think and to what extent you may be able to drive them in the pursuit of a goal. Frequently, we see people paralysed by unachievable deadlines or targets set by upper management – simply because someone had a great idea of how to make more money without knowing if the people responsible for achieving these new goals were mentally or emotionally prepared to do so.

*Don't fear failure so much
that you refuse to try new things.
The saddest summary of a life
contains three descriptions: could
have, might have, and should have.*

~

Louis E. Boone

INNOVATION

Innovation refers to the generation of new ideas, the tenacity to bring the best ones to life and the wisdom to know how to enthuse others to support them.

Innovation involves expanding our mind and the understanding of how to draw on our own and others' ingrained ability to imagine. Implementing innovations at team and organisational levels also requires the vision and the stamina to move ahead without getting discouraged while juggling other short-term priorities.

WHAT TO LOOK FOR IN A PERSON →

HIGH INNOVATION

- ✓ Is able to take a leap of faith even in uncertain situations
- ✓ Sees patterns and makes connections easily
- ✓ Is always willing to offer alternative solutions
- ✓ Considers problems as an opportunity
- ✓ Does not give up easily
- ✓ Is eager to explore, learn and change what does not work
- ✓ Takes responsibility
- ✓ Usually expects the best
- ✓ Is persistent
- ✓ Knows when to let go and doesn't take things personally

LOW INNOVATION

- ✗ Is not willing to risk anything
- ✗ Lacks the confidence to try new things
- ✗ Is satisfied with what he/she knows and the way things are
- ✗ Places high value on tradition
- ✗ Lacks resilience and energy
- ✗ Is firmly grounded in his/her beliefs
- ✗ Is cautious and sceptical
- ✗ Is more inclined to think that 'it won't work'
- ✗ Is not resourceful

*If you want something new,
you have to stop doing
something old.*

~

Peter Drucker

THE PILLARS OF INNOVATION ➡

Innovation has become one of the strategic imperatives for organisations around the world.

In addition, the recent discoveries about how our brains function whenever a creative moment occurs have shed new light on how anyone can access their creative thinking, be innovative and become part of more dynamic workplaces where people are seen as co-creators, rather than passive observers.

The pillars of Innovation are: Imagination, Drive, Curiosity and Attitude.

In the following sections, you will be able to learn what these four pillars refer to within the context of the i4 Model.

IMAGINATION

Imagination is the faculty of mentally forming new concepts, ideas or patterns without involving the senses.

Imaginative people take the time to reach into the depth of their stored knowledge, assemble the pieces of information in new ways, examine the various combinations and imagine or visualise how they will play out in new conditions. There are three aspects that help to define the pillar of imagination:

DAYDREAMING

Daydreaming occurs when our minds drift away from the present moment and the focus is no longer on the external environment.

A wandering mind has always been associated with 'wasting' time, a belief that is now being challenged by new research. These findings suggest that our minds wander between 20-50% of the time, depending on the task we are doing. When we daydream, our brains are able to imagine future possibilities, remember the past, link disparate concepts, and consider both our own and others' thoughts, feelings and perspectives.

When our minds wander, a complex series of neural connections called the 'default network', which includes parts of the prefrontal cortex and the hippocampus, become active while other brain regions turn off.

In relation to leadership

As critical as it is to spend part of our awake time focusing on a particular task whilst reducing distractions, according to an article published in the *Journal of Psychological Science* daydreaming is a mental activity that can help a person produce more answers to problems than the act of pure concentration.

A more useful mindset to have, as a leader, is to be aware that team members who at times drift away are not necessarily wasting their time, but perhaps contemplating other ways of looking at a situation to come up with creative solutions. It is also worth noting that the brain's ability to daydream reduces with age and in those who suffer from dementia and Alzheimer's disease.

IDEAS GENERATION

Inventions, discoveries and ideas generated by the human mind have always existed, despite the fact that for a long time many have believed that creativity was the gift of a select few.

The power to imagine and the potential to innovate exists within all of us. The appetite to express our creativity has rapidly expanded throughout our virtual world with new creations in the fields of music, poetry and video, with artworks emerging from the most remote places on earth – an incredible phenomenon never before experienced.

Creative thinking is the mental process of generating new ideas, some of which are original – such as the creation of new business models like the Amazon platform, which changed the way people purchased books and other goods.

In the last 7 to 10 years, researchers like American neuroscientist Mark Jung-Beeman have made important discoveries to help understand how the creative brain works, how our mental state and mood affect creativity and how to increase our potential for the generation of ideas. These new findings are revolutionising the way people look at creativity in both their professional and personal lives.

In relation to leadership

Knowing that we can be more creative when we access a slower form of brain waves through relaxation (having a shower, travelling by train) and when we are in a good mood, has redefined the way some organisations and leaders promote a culture of creativity and growth (rather than repression and constraint).

Examples of this are companies like Google, Dropbox, Twitter, Atlassian and Menlo Innovations, where the focus on results is high, but so is the focus on play, physical and mental well-being and true collaboration, with the aim of having an arena to evaluate options and pick the best idea to implement.

New research suggests that performing common tasks in unusual ways, taking notes of your dreams when you wake up and making time to re-think an issue while playing a game of ping-pong are some of the things you can do to boost your creative powers.

PATTERN RECOGNITION

As described in the 'certainty' component of Dr. David Rock's SCARF Model, our brains are like pattern-recognition machines that are continuously trying to predict the near future.

The information we receive from our external environment through touch, sight, taste, smell and hearing is processed in different regions and networks in the brain, with the purpose of finding 'meaning' in our experience. This new data is automatically compared with previous memories and in combination with our intuition and judgment, we recognise patterns and decide what to do next.

In relation to leadership

Fine-tuning our powers of observation and paying attention to the thoughts that emerge from these mental processes can improve one's ability to recognise patterns. Sometimes, in business, people get caught up in dealing with operational issues and become obsessed with deadlines, targets and details.

However, by scanning the environment for new things, recognising patterns and being open to discussing what could be possible, we can help enhance our strategic ability, useful in thinking about 'outside the box' solutions for future scenarios.

Life has a funny way of testing you to see if you really want, what you say you want.

~

Turcois Ominek

DRIVE

Drive refers to having the strength and perseverance to pursue the actions required in order to attain a desired goal.

In combination with hard work, creativity and optimism, drive is an essential ingredient to convert ideas into reality. There are three aspects that help to define the pillar of drive:

OPTIMISM

Being optimistic means having the best or most positive expectation about an outcome or future situation. It's also known as seeing the glass 'half full' instead of 'half empty'.

The reason why someone is optimistic rather than pessimistic has been widely studied by psychologists. These studies reveal that the way in which our brains interpret the world may affect how we live our lives and in turn, how we respond to the adverse situations we face each day.

Monitoring our internal thoughts and noticing our biases towards what happens in our environment can be instrumental in changing ourselves and developing a more positive disposition.

In relation to leadership

Optimistic people exude an energy that attracts others. On the other hand, working for negative (or pessimistic) bosses who complain, whine and cannot envision the solution to a problem is hard and is likely to make most team members refrain from trusting or feeling inspired.

Developing an optimistic approach to life is unrivalled if we are to spot opportunities and generate the energy to move forward. Leaders who are optimistic are keen to drive new projects, communicate openly and elicit enthusiasm from others to awaken the spirit of innovation that any team or organisation needs.

RESILIENCE

Life can bring all sorts of setbacks – illnesses, deaths, romantic break-ups, job or financial losses – which are part of our human existence.

The capacity to cope and recover from the emotional trauma of any of these major events (or even minor ones) is called resilience.

Individuals with higher levels of resilience can better manage their fears and emotions and are also able to change their frame of reference when it comes to negative life situations and minimise the stress that can arise in those circumstances.

In relation to leadership

Months after the 2008 global financial crisis, numerous organisations rediscovered the forgotten notion of being resilient, quickly and reactively organising training workshops for their leaders to learn how to develop this capacity.

As useful as a one-day workshop can be in terms of creating awareness, resilience is a complex response which changes from person to person, depending significantly on how each person's brain networks are wired and how different regions interact with one another. Understanding the biological underpinnings of resilience can help create more effective interventions to assist leaders to overcome adversity and navigate difficult times in business and in life.

DETERMINATION

Determination involves having both the confidence and the willpower to pursue a specific outcome.

This is as critical to innovation as how strongly we believe in our ideas. Many extraordinary ideas are sometimes left behind due to a lack of perseverance by those who generated them. In regards to willpower, the latest neuroscience findings reveal that the will to do something depends on what takes place in our prefrontal cortex (PFC).

The left part of the PFC helps us stick to the difficult tasks, while the right part inhibits the distractions that may derail us. One of the most important findings is that we have a finite supply of willpower and our determination is likely to rely on the ability to focus on the one new thing we want to achieve.

In relation to leadership

The most successful leaders have a clear goal; they stick to it, work hard and are relentless in its pursuit. At the same time, they are able to ignore those who tell them that it is too difficult to be achieved or it is not worth the effort.

Some of the most memorable and influential people throughout history — Gandhi, Abraham Lincoln, Steve Jobs, Estee Lauder, Bill Gates, Eva Peron and Coco Chanel — have been known to have a fierce determination in all of the feats they undertook. While many give up along the way, it is those who insist that their ideas are worth listening to, who are the ones that have a chance to influence and change the status quo.

*Motivation is a fire from within.
If someone else tries to light that fire
under you, chances are it will burn
very briefly.*

~

Stephen Covey

CURIOSITY

Curiosity refers to the thirst for knowing and the desire to explore and learn.

An eager and open mind can help a person see alternative options that are invisible to the eyes of others, to improve what currently exists. There are three aspects that help to define the pillar of curiosity:

EAGERNESS TO LEARN

Information is now widely available to anyone who can access a computer. Being able to learn new skills, provide and exchange opinions has swiftly altered the concept of learning, creating an appetite for acquiring knowledge that was previously limited to those who had the economic resources to do so.

The methods and technologies to access content and interact with subject matter experts are awakening the eagerness to learn, an important mindset to have in times when constantly changing economies are requiring people to look for several new jobs throughout their working lives.

In relation to leadership
Organisations that support their leaders and staff to grow and create a culture of learning instead of slashing training budgets are more sustainable and able to retain talent in times of crisis.

As a leader, showing interest in what a staff member has learnt after going to a training program and asking them how they can apply this new information ensures more engagement and a positive attitude towards learning.

INQUISITIVE NATURE

Inquisitiveness is one of the traits that has pushed humans to leap from one discovery to another.

Asking questions and demonstrating an inclination to investigate are essential aspects of curiosity. These traits can mark the difference between those who achieve and those who believe that they can stick around forever doing the same thing.

In the past, people were accustomed to having one job for life, and being inquisitive was perhaps less relevant than it is today. Market conditions have changed dramatically and having staff members who are willing to go the extra mile is something that any employer looks for.

In relation to leadership

Working with people who are inquisitive would certainly challenge more traditional and compliant managers, who may feel uncomfortable dealing with a constant influx of questions and information and may not possess the flexibility to take it in.

On the other end of the spectrum, a leader who works well with curious people will benefit from having an open mind, a willingness to listen and an ability to discern what information can be useful.

HONESTY

Being honest means not deceiving, lying, cheating or doing things that could potentially affect others negatively.

Honesty is the basis of trusting relationships and when asked, most people expect honesty from those whom they come into contact with. However, it seems that in humans, lying or cheating, even a little, is more common than everyone thinks.

According to research by a number of behavioural economists, including best-selling author Dan Ariely, the potential for loss can increase the motivation to cheat and this may lead people to put aside their honesty and ethics.

In relation to leadership

Being asked to work with unethical leaders would probably mean declining such a job offer. When given a choice, the preference for most people would be to work for a leader who is honest and has high ethical standards. Everyone intuitively knows that in the long term, dishonesty is neither good for the individual nor for society.

In reality, current work practices seem to ignore the importance of instructing staff on ethical behaviour and promoting reward systems that reinforce the right behaviours. Culture is usually defined as 'the way we do things here'. It is made up of a set of behaviours, processes and systems that create the expected outcomes. When a leader sets the example, he or she creates the culture – so it is obvious that honest leaders have a better chance of creating honest cultures.

We keep moving forward, opening new doors and doing new things because we are curious and curiosity keeps leading us down new paths.

~

Walt Disney

ATTITUDE

Attitude refers to the willingness to embrace doing things differently and a positive disposition towards experimentation.

Being proactive and expecting the best outcomes while embracing change are the foundation stones that allow an innovative mindset to emerge. There are three aspects that help to define the pillar of attitude:

POSITIVITY

Positivity means having more pleasant than unpleasant feelings in regards to what we experience in our lives.

How we feel is a consequence of the combined emotional reactions that cascade throughout our brains and bodies and the thoughts we have. When we pay attention to what we are thinking, we can recognise if our thoughts are mostly negative (or even unhealthy) or if they are positive. When we think positively, we feel keen to embrace the possibilities and look for solutions.

If our thoughts are mostly negative, it is likely we will start to judge other people's ideas or opinions and assume things about a situation or a person that may be different from reality. The way we think determines how happy or unhappy we are in relation to the things we do and the interactions we have. Cultivating positive thinking, challenging the negative patterns and adjusting the words we use are essential for expanding our opportunities and overcoming the hurdles along the way.

In relation to leadership

When people are led towards a goal, they expect quite a lot from their leader. Even in small teams, a leader sets the pace, models the behaviours, establishes the priorities and sets the moral compass.

The expectations are certainly big and the efforts can be derailed easily when the leader becomes negative, blames, criticises, uses language that is undermining rather than constructive and thinks of the worst outcomes in moments of crisis.

On the other hand, leaders who are positive, encouraging and do not lose their positivity during critical moments are able to gain the respect, help and support of their followers when implementing solutions and carrying out demanding projects.

EMBRACING CHANGE

As most people would have experienced throughout their lives, change is constant.

When change occurs, some of us embrace it easily, while others resist it. It is now known in the neuroscientific field that change requires conscious effort, as it involves the executive part of the brain prioritising and working out the new habits that have to be developed in order to adjust to the change.

When we are accustomed to doing things in a specific way, these long-term habits are stored in the middle part of our brains in the areas called basal ganglia and hippocampus. Creating new habits demands attention and effort and for some people this is more difficult than for others.

Keeping the brain flexible and continuously incorporating new habits and learning new things helps the brain to grow new neural connections that can assist us to embrace change.

In relation to leadership

Leaders who embrace change in a positive manner and take into account the insights of how the brain responds to it, are better positioned to influence others to do the same. Building awareness, selling the benefits, making it personal, providing the end vision and keeping people focused on what needs to be done, are all skills and abilities that a leader can use to reinforce the attitude needed to make innovation become a second-nature mindset, instead of a one-off or casual activity.

PROACTIVITY

In 1989, when American author Stephen Covey released his best-selling book "The 7 Habits of Highly Effective People", he established "Being Proactive" as the first one of these habits.

Being proactive was defined by Covey as the notion of "taking initiative by realising that our decisions are the primary determining factor for effectiveness in our lives." Since the release of Covey's book, much has been discovered in regards to how our brain's functioning influences the choices or decisions we make.

Although the principle of being proactive is a great mindset to have in the pursuit of innovation, understanding the underlying mechanisms of having a healthy brain (including its chemistry) has become even more relevant.

In relation to leadership

Working for reactive or laid back leaders can be quite de-motivating and disengaging. Proactive leaders, on the other hand, inspire and motivate others to have the desire to do things and to innovate. Proactivity creates movement, and with movement, goals are achieved and feelings of satisfaction start to emerge.

It is also imperative for a leader to explore what may be happening to a team member who does not show any signs of being proactive. Excessive stress, personal problems or unhealthy habits can inhibit a person's willingness to engage and act.

Proactivity, however, does not imply being 'always active'. At times, it may be more effective for a leader to stop, reflect, consider the bigger picture and start a discussion with his or her team about what the next steps should be, rather than just being proactive for the sake of it.

What is the difference between an obstacle and an opportunity? Our attitude toward it. Every opportunity has a difficulty and every difficulty has an opportunity.

~

J. Sidlow Baxter

AGILITY

Agility refers to the capacity to read changing conditions in one's environment and the ability to rapidly adapt to them.

Leadership agility refers to the good use we make of our intuitive abilities, the awareness of self and our capacity to observe and reflect. Agility is also linked to how well we can influence others to navigate complex and uncertain environments and our degree of adaptation to new conditions.

WHAT TO LOOK FOR IN A PERSON ➡

HIGH AGILITY

- ✓ Is mindful and aware of self and his/her environment
- ✓ Acts quickly
- ✓ Can influence others easily
- ✓ Is willing to change
- ✓ Trusts his/her instincts
- ✓ Notices what needs to be done and acts on it
- ✓ Can easily change course and implement new measures
- ✓ Understands people
- ✓ Conveys an aura of certainty
- ✓ Has personal power

LOW AGILITY

- ✗ Has self-doubt
- ✗ Is unwilling to compromise
- ✗ Cannot cope with ambiguity and complexity
- ✗ Gets stuck if things are too difficult to assimilate
- ✗ Relies on rules and authority
- ✗ Has difficulty in making things happen
- ✗ Has to go through facts and information in order to feel certain
- ✗ Is slow to act
- ✗ Does not know how to guide others
- ✗ Is highly structured

*It is through science that we prove,
but through intuition that
we discover.*

~

Henri Poincaré

THE PILLARS OF AGILITY →

In a complex world where uncertainty and change are constant factors, agility has indisputably become one of the prime competencies to develop.

Being agile can help people anticipate and solve issues that appear more often in rapidly changing environments. It can also assist leaders in bringing others along when there is resistance to the new conditions.

The pillars of Agility are: Intuition, Awareness, Influence and Adaptability.

In the sections that follow, you will learn what these 4 pillars refer to within the context of the i4 Model.

INTUITION

Intuition refers to the ability to know something without the involvement of conscious reasoning.

As we learn new pieces of information, we start to recognise patterns and if this happens regularly, these bits of data become organised into blocks of knowledge, which are stored in our long-term memory. There are three aspects that help to define the pillar of intuition:

INTUITIVE INSIGHTS

Rational thinking, analysis and domination have been the primary drivers of the way things are done within organisations.

This has limited the belief that intuition is a worthwhile, innate ability to utilise when it comes to work matters. Intuitive insights are useful pieces of information which can definitely be taken into account in our work activities.

All humans have the capacity to intuit and connect to the intelligence of our hearts and guts, which can lead us in the right direction, often even more than the cognitive and subjective information that emerges from our mental processing.

In relation to leadership
Leaders who learn to connect with their intuition are in a better position to deal with uncertainty, chaos and multiple sources of information.

Intuitive leaders are good at recognising patterns, anticipating trends and having confidence and insights – essential traits for the modern age. Intuition is an ability that can be developed and fine-tuned, particularly if judgments and assumptions are restricted and full attention is given to the 'inner voice' that we all possess.

DECISION-MAKING

Whether we are driving a car; dancing to our favourite tune; playing guitar while talking to our best friend; or typing an email response, we are constantly making split decisions without being conscious of them.

The belief (and almost obsession) that has dominated the minds of those who have worked for organisations throughout the industrial and knowledge era supports the fact that the best decisions are the ones that can be proven with data, graphs and statistics, all logically arranged to be assimilated and accepted by the rational parts of our brains.

Although neuroscientists, like Antonio Damasio and many others, have disproved the point that decisions are made purely with our rational minds, the myth still continues and paperwork, justifications and logic are very much required to get the approval of those who have the last say.

In relation to leadership

Now, imagine people talking to their leaders, sharing their intuitive insights and discussing them openly before choosing the best ones so they can then be analysed with the tools or methods that are currently used. Wouldn't it be better for leaders to have some of this 'extra' information, and wouldn't team members be more engaged simply because they are able to express how they feel in regards to a particular decision?

In the field of emotional intelligence, one of the skills to learn (based on the Genos Model developed by Australian Dr. Ben Palmer), is that of making decisions based on both emotions and cognition. Entrepreneurs and business leaders like Richard Branson are known to talk about intuition openly. I believe it is time for intuition to be accepted as a valuable source of information in the business world.

SENSE OF 'KNOWING'

Within the new field of neuro-gastroenterology, the medical profession is focused on studying the gut, the brain and their interactions, mainly with the purpose of discovering the reasons for gastrointestinal disorders.

Even though most of us often use the term 'gut feeling' to describe an intuitive or emotional response, very few know how both affect each other and what this means in terms of our responses to stress.

This renewed interest in the gut – now called the second brain – may provide insights into how the enteric nervous system and the gut neurons – 500 million of them – produce the feelings of 'knowing' that we all experience on a frequent basis.

In relation to leadership

As a result of leading-edge scientific research and the work of those keen to apply the latest knowledge to organisational practices such as coaching, a new methodology has emerged.

Developed by behavioural modellers and Neuro-Linguistic Programming experts Marvin Oka and Grant Soosalu (www.mbraining.com), this coaching method consists of learning how to integrate all three neural networks, known as the three brains: head, gut and heart.

What these experts have done is to come up with a new way of thinking and working with the body's intelligence in order to transform how people process the information from their environment, so they can have a more coherent and healthy response to work and life challenges.

We are undoubtedly changing the way we value our abilities and how we operate as human beings; it is not only about tapping into our cognitive abilities, but also knowing how to integrate the wisdom that our bodies have to offer, and coaching is no exception.

The art of being wise is the art of knowing what to overlook.

~

William James

AWARENESS

Awareness refers to the ability to perceive and become conscious of one's inner world, while also noticing what takes place in our external environment.

Developing mindfulness, which includes learning to pay attention, observe and understand the impact of our reactions, strengths and weaknesses, can significantly influence the way we respond to others. Neuroscientists investigating consciousness are concluding that awareness emerges when information travels back and forth between different brain areas and is not just restricted to the frontal lobes. There are three aspects that help to define the pillar of awareness:

MINDFULNESS

Being 'mindful' means to be aware of one's present thoughts, emotions, and actions. This capacity increases the likelihood of managing our state to be more effective.

By utilising neuroscientific methods, mindful meditation has been proven to increase the ability to be more present, have better self-control, reduce stress and depression, and boost working memory.

In relation to leadership
The demands that leaders (and people in general) are subject to, in today's working environments, have triggered greater-than-ever levels of job stress. This has consequences in terms of more health-related issues and associated costs.

We have more and more scientific information and empirical evidence at our fingertips that demonstrates that we can improve our well-being by simply taking a few minutes each day to practice mindful meditation; this practice needs to reach everyone in our societies and be included as part of our daily routines.

OPEN TO FEEDBACK

Seeking feedback is as simple as asking others to describe how they see or perceive us.

Adopting this practice on a regular basis can give us insights that otherwise would be missed, as our brains can take in only partial information and from that, they can only derive limited conclusions.

Feedback can also affirm what we are doing right and how others are impacted by our actions. Asking for feedback from those who know us well is a way of making sense of the reality outside our heads and in turn, give us more tools to enhance our overall performance.

In relation to leadership

New developments in the area of neuro-feedback have demonstrated that providing the brain with real-time feedback helps the brain to optimise its functioning. In the same way, when people receive feedback from others, if the feedback is framed properly, people have an opportunity to improve their understanding of themselves and how others perceive them.

Anyone who wants to be better at a particular sport would engage a coach to get feedback on their performance. In business, however, people have come to believe that coaching and feedback are to be used only on occasions or at certain levels within an organisation. Seeking and receiving feedback surely can help advance one's career and expand our capacity to lead, negotiate, communicate and interact with others.

PERIPHERAL VISION

Peripheral vision allows us to have a visual sense of what is taking place in our surroundings.

Without it, we would have a view limited only to what happens directly in front of us and would miss out on other important information from the environment.

This extra element of visual awareness is often overlooked, however psychologists and scientists are studying it and revealing new strategies on how we can improve it.

We know that peripheral vision can decrease with age, although it can also be re-trained and even expanded due to brain plasticity. Driving a car, reading a book, playing sports, knowing what happens around the office and noticing people's facial expressions all depend on this ability.

In relation to leadership

Considering that non-verbal language makes up more than 80% of the communication flow, and words only represent a small percentage of the message, being able to see and use any other piece of extra information can help us identify the roadblocks, objections and dissatisfaction that a client, peer or member of our own team may have.

Leaders who are observant can notice and see beyond what most people see, have the upper-hand when it comes to conducting effective negotiations or meetings in general, as they can capture the data that most other people would miss.

It's all a matter of paying attention, being awake in the present moment, and not expecting a huge payoff. The magic in this world seems to work in whispers and small kindnesses.

~

Charles de Lint

INFLUENCE

Influence refers to a person's capacity to have an effect on other people or situations.

Successfully guiding others towards a goal or vision requires a set of well-developed skills along with respect, passion and conviction. There are three aspects that help to define the pillar of influence:

PERSONAL POWER

Throughout history, power has defined relationships between people.

The majority of people link the word 'power' with possessing physical strength, having special knowledge or occupying a high position within a hierarchy.

Since 2002, the ease of access to technology and social media platforms has added the possibility of 'creating and displaying', which has generated a different type of power, defined by the character traits, talent or ideas that a person possesses (personal power) and the ability to market them. The thought of personal power, although it has existed previously, has now become more potent and is a novel way of adding value to the economy while influencing others to follow.

In relation to leadership

It is hard to imagine a leader today trying to exercise his or her positional power on younger people who think radically differently from the way people did thirty years ago.
The opportunities that exist for anyone to take the lead, have a say and build a brand or product that the market wants are unprecedented. The world is undergoing a major transformation, with new markets and new players from different cultures, generations and ideas - a phenomenon never seen before.

Organisations and leaders who can see this new reality and come up with ways of attracting people who have personal power will be the winners in the years to come.

CLEAR PRIORITIES

Learning to set priorities in terms of goals and tasks helps people to focus on what needs to be done and when. This provides the direction that is required to accomplish what's been agreed to, in terms of bigger objectives.

Setting priorities provides the stimulus and moves people into action. It is important though, to take into account the abilities, resources, time and level of commitment that are available when establishing these priorities.

In relation to leadership

Although there are many methods to set clear priorities, keeping in mind how the brain best responds is a more effective way of looking at this topic. Using the Herrmann Brain Dominance Instrument (created by American researcher Ned Herrmann) can easily give us a clue into how others may respond to prioritisation.

The Ideas Person

Gets enthused by understanding the big picture and imagining future possibilities.

Establish priorities by giving an overall explanation of what the vision is about and what has to happen first, keeping the details to a minimum.

The People Person

Responds to stories, feelings, informal contact and being part of a team.

Establish priorities by paying attention to their intuition and what they feel is the best way of going about it. It is better to talk through things 'with' them rather than just telling them what to do.

The Analytical Person

Prefers straightforward and rational arguments and a linear and logical format to follow.

Establish priorities by classifying what is urgent and what is important.
They will act on what is a priority if it makes sense without wasting too much time.

The Organised Person

Responds better to sequential, planned and well organised procedures.

Establish priorities by creating to-do lists and a detailed schedule and process of how to achieve each of them.

RESPECT

The feeling of wanting to be respected, acknowledged and recognised for our ideas and achievements has not yet disappeared from our biology.

Nevertheless, in today's work environments, the lack of respect is quite noticeable. This aspect, that many simply accept as part of doing business, is re-shaping how people interact with one another, sometimes in ways that are less than desirable.

In relation to leadership

As important as it is to have mutual respect between leaders and followers, the notion of respect has become less 'top of mind' in a world where the norm is electronic communication and virtual interactions. This has gradually affected people's social ability.

Learning how to gain respect and giving respect back to others, however, are the basic ingredients of being a great influencer, so perhaps we all need to start teaching and relearning what respect looks like and its importance.

The key to successful leadership is influence, not authority.

~

Kenneth H. Blanchard

ADAPTABILITY

Adaptability refers to the ability to adjust effectively to changes in one's environment.

The ability to remain flexible, modify the course of action when faced with ambiguous situations and to accept the unexpected, are at the core of adapting to changing conditions at work and in life. There are three aspects that help to define the pillar of adaptability:

VERSATILITY

Versatility is about being flexible and getting used to new situations and environments quickly.

While change may be uncomfortable, experts say that it is possible. Due to the process of neuroplasticity, the brain is able to 'rewire itself'. Neuroplasticity is seen as one of the biggest breakthroughs in the field of neuroscience.

It is now known that the brain is malleable and continuously grows new cells and connections. Every part of the brain can rewire in direct response to what we think, see and do, independent of age.

In relation to leadership

One of the biggest challenges for leaders in organisations is influencing people to accept and move through major reorganisations, shifts in business strategies and other initiatives that involve significant changes.

Even though resistance is natural, particularly when change is imposed, knowing that our brains can shift, adapt and think differently provides renewed hope when it comes to navigating the constant changes that affect today's workplaces.

A leader can support others by explaining how and why change works, by learning to regulate his or her own emotions more effectively and by having the tough conversations in a brain-friendly manner.

DEALING WITH UNCERTAINTY

Anyone who lives in our interconnected world has probably heard this statement: "We live in uncertain times".

Uncertainty and how we feel about it may not be that different to how it was experienced by our ancestors. Our bodies are prepared to deal with uncertain scenarios by increasing our heart rate, making plenty of energy available and by secreting adrenaline or noradrenaline for us to either run away or stay and fight (referred to as the flight or fight reaction).

In relation to leadership

It is now quite well known that our brains are more similar to pattern-prediction machines than to organisms that prefer chaotic scenarios. Chaos amplifies discomfort, creating emotions that can make people freeze, flee or fight.

Uncertainty can be mind-numbing, disorienting and it can undermine people's confidence, making the executive part of the brain (prefrontal cortex) work harder to find the solutions to problems whenever conditions change. Leaders within organisations underestimate the consequences of change and usually lack the expertise to communicate and help others to navigate through it.

SELF-CORRECTION

Self-correction is the ability to look within and assess how we conduct ourselves in the activities that we undertake in both our personal and professional lives.

From the moment we are born, we learn though repetition with groups of neurons in our brains connecting with each other innumerable times. This constant action helps us develop the habits that condition how we act, see the world and approach situations.

In relation to leadership

In leadership development, learning to self-reflect and seeking feedback from others are the first steps towards influencing and leading others successfully. These two actions can assist in one's self-evaluation of behaviours and in understanding the impact we have on others.

There is a myriad of useful strategies and many books written on this subject that can assist leaders in reshaping certain mental processes and patterns that when improved, can result in better leadership performance.

It is not the strongest or the most intelligent who will survive but those who can best manage change.

~

Charles Darwin

Chapter Seven

INTEGRATION

DON'T LET YOUR MIND BULLY YOUR BODY INTO BELIEVING IT MUST CARRY THE BURDEN OF ITS WORRIES.

Astrid Alauda

WHEN JUDGMENT GOES WRONG

At 1:35 a.m. on June 1, 2009, having left Rio de Janeiro three hours earlier and en route to Paris, Air France Flight 447 with its 228 passengers and crew on board plunged into the Atlantic Ocean and disappeared within a matter of minutes.

Two years and $30 million later, after undertaking the difficult task of scanning the bottom of the sea, the plane's black box was found and the mystery of why the plane crashed started to unravel.

It was hard to believe for any of the investigators, both French authorities and Air France personnel, how a state-of-the-art Airbus 330, with the latest electronic safety and navigation features could have dropped from the sky, taking all on board to an unexpected and sudden death.

In July 2012, the final report revealed that the aircraft crashed after inconsistencies between airspeed measurements, due to the external pilot tubes being obstructed by ice crystals, caused the autopilot to disconnect and subsequently prompted the crew to react incorrectly. The series of events led the aircraft to an aerodynamic stall that none of the three pilots involved were able to reverse.

Months after the official report, more frightening revelations hit the news about the pilots' lack of sleep. The voice of the main pilot, Captain Dubois, was recorded telling the co-pilot that he had not had enough sleep.

After the investigations were completed, it was also made public that he had been on a weekend away in Rio with his girlfriend, who was an off-duty flight attendant working for the same airline.

We will never know whether everyone on board could have escaped their fatal destiny if there had not been judgment errors and the pilots had realised how to prevent such a fast descent.

What is probably more useful to think about is how the human brain performs at its best, not only in life-and-death situations but also in daily decision-making and when we interact with others, strategise or implement plans.

With regards to the importance of sleep and productivity, there is extensive research that explains the link between having a good night's sleep or a short nap during the day and the fulfilment of daily tasks.

Insufficient sleep increases irritability, reduces attention and limits the ability to respond to complex issues. In business, however, this fact is completely ignored when it comes to asking pilots, truck drivers, emergency doctors or others in professions that demand high levels of attention to work extended hours with the aim of reducing costs and without any consideration for the potential consequences.

Jessica Payne, a neuroscientist at the University of Notre Dame's Sleep, Stress and Memory Lab, predicts that some day people will take a short nap at work, knowing they will be more productive for the rest of the day. Some companies, such as Google, have already conducted sleep awareness programs and added sleeping pods for people to take brief naps at work.

Even when other professions or jobs may not carry the same level of risk, it is known that the brain works better when it has the appropriate amount of rest.

So to those of you who think you can perform at your best with little sleep, think again.

Sleep is not the only aspect that helps to keep the brain balanced and working optimally.

Neuroscientists are beginning to understand the complex mechanisms that underpin the different brain systems, its neural networks and the intricate connections between the left and the right hemispheres. It is these findings that will probably inform us how to better use our brains in ways we never thought possible.

WHAT IS INTEGRATION?

Defining 'integration' is not a simple task as the word is currently used in different ways. Below are a couple of examples:

- At the School of Biomedical Sciences, University of Queensland, Australia, a subject called "The Integrated Brain" has been offered since 2010. The course focuses on learning how different brain systems work together in an integrated fashion.

- Dr. Daniel Siegel, clinical professor of psychiatry at the UCLA School of Medicine and founding co-director of the Mindful Awareness Research Centre, refers to the importance of integrating the two hemispheres of the brain. He explains that when people live mostly using the left side of the brain (the more logical, analytical and linear type of processing), they become cut off from their feelings and imagery of dreams, may lose context and become rigid.

  In contrast, people who are using the right side of the brain, without the balance of the left, may become flooded by their feelings, being constantly aware of every sensation they have. These people may need to do relaxation exercises to calm these excessive reactions. According to Dr. Siegel, a person who wants to live a balanced life and be creative, calm and compassionate, is someone who is able to integrate both sides of the brain without shutting down their feelings or becoming overwhelmed by them.

- The brain is a sophisticated organ that involves many parts working well together, somewhat like an orchestra, where all the instruments are playing in tune. In healthy brain scans, the brain shows full, even symmetrical activity, and according to Dr. Daniel Amen:

  "People are happier, healthier, wiser and more successful when they have healthy and balanced brains."

  One extremely useful method for exploring leadership behaviour is to understand in more depth how the different brain systems work and how their optimal and suboptimal functioning is reflected in a person's actions

"

WHEN YOUR BRAIN WORKS RIGHT, YOU WORK RIGHT. WHEN YOUR
BRAIN DOESN'T WORK RIGHT, YOU CAN'T WORK RIGHT.

Dr. Daniel Amen

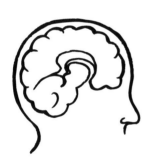

BRAIN SYSTEMS

In the next pages you will find a short description of the five main brain systems and their relationship to people's behaviours, based on the Amen Clinics classification of brain systems. Used with their kind permission: www.amenclinics.com

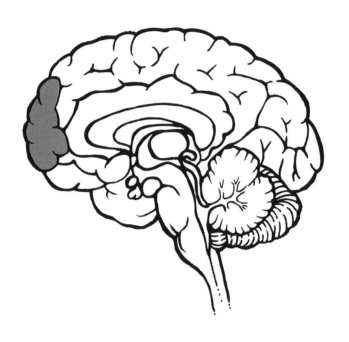

PRE-FRONTAL CORTEX (PFC)

Front tip of the brain, behind the forehead.

When it works well – optimal behaviours:

People can focus their attention, have a clear sense of what they want to achieve, are empathetic and can manage their impulses. They also demonstrate common sense, good judgment, are more creative and able to realise their mistakes.

When it does not work well – suboptimal behaviours:

People tend to procrastinate, avoid making decisions or make the wrong ones. They may cancel appointments without considering the repercussions, become distracted in meetings, lack empathy or be oblivious to the impact they have on others. They may also lack creative thinking, be disorganised and pay insufficient attention to detail.

⊕   *This illustration is an approximate visual representation*

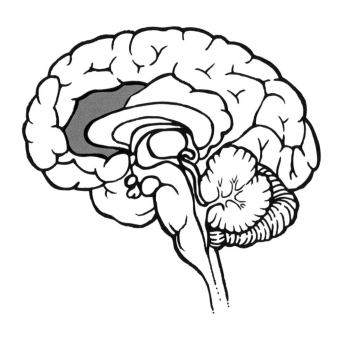

ANTERIOR CINGULATE GYRUS

Part of the brain that runs longitudinally through the middle part of the frontal lobes.

When it works well – optimal behaviours:
People have cognitive flexibility, are cooperative and able to adapt more easily to change, as they are more able to perceive a number of options.

When it does not work well – suboptimal behaviours:
In this case, people may have a tendency to be argumentative and oppositional. They dislike change and are easily worried, may say no without thinking and can become inflexible, self-centred and obsessive. They seem to have more negative than positive thinking patterns.

⊕   *This illustration is an approximate visual representation*

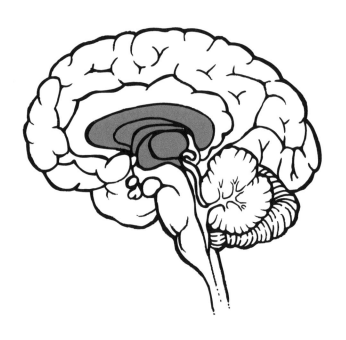

DEEP LIMBIC SYSTEM

At the centre of the brain.

When it works well – optimal behaviours:
People are motivated and energised, connect well with others and have a moderate flight or fight response.

When it does not work well – suboptimal behaviours:
In this case, people can be easily irritated, have low motivation and a tendency to blame themselves or others. They may become sad, depressed or socially disconnected.

⊙ *This illustration is an approximate visual representation*

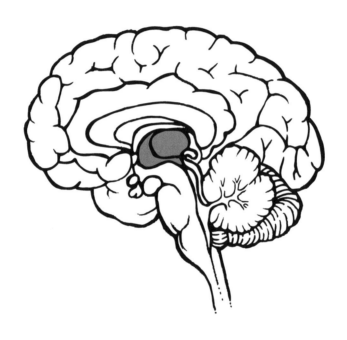

BASAL GANGLIA

Deep structures within the brain.

When it works well – optimal behaviours:
People are able to integrate their thoughts and feelings, modulating their moods effectively.

When it does not work well – suboptimal behaviours:
In this case, people may avoid conflict, predict the worst or have an excessive motivation to work (workaholics). They may also experience muscle tension, becoming anxious and freezing in difficult situations.

⊕ *This illustration is an approximate visual representation*

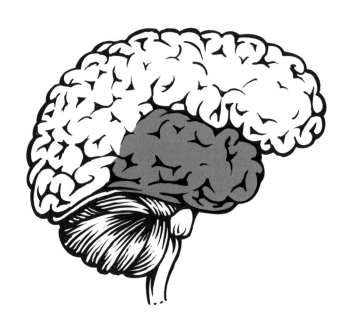

TEMPORAL LOBES

Underneath the temples and behind the eyes.

When they work well – optimal behaviours:

These people enjoy good long-term memory (it seems easier for them to remember words), have a sense of music and rhythm and an excellent understanding of language.

When it does not work well – suboptimal behaviours:

In this case, people may experience memory problems and poor auditory processing. They have difficulties in finding the right word and are prone to rapid mood swings. If the left temporal lobe is affected, it may be problematic for people to read social cues and they may misinterpret what others say. If the right temporal lobe is not functioning properly, people may be easily angered and show aggressiveness towards others. Issues with the right temporal lobe have also been linked to dyslexia.

⊕   *This illustration is an approximate visual representation*

LEADERSHIP & BRAIN INTEGRATION

Being aware of these behaviours offers a new level of understanding when it comes to the multifaceted art and science of leadership.

For more information on how to identify and optimise the brain systems, refer to the book "Change Your Brain, Change Your Life", by Dr. Daniel Amen.

Taking care of our brain's performance has become as important as taking care of the day-to-day tasks we have to do.

Being effective in today's world of work requires adapting to new circumstances, rethinking processes, being aware of market conditions and having the ability to quickly connect with unfamiliar colleagues in order to complete a project successfully.

To do all of this is extremely demanding for anyone's brain, but it can be even more challenging for those whose brains are functioning at a less-than-optimal level.

Understanding the importance of developing an integrated brain and its relationship with leadership effectiveness is being researched and studied by many, among them — Dr. Harald Harung (Associate Professor at Norway's Oslo and Akershus University College of Applied Sciences) and Dr. Fred Travis (Director of the Centre for Brain, Consciousness and Cognition, Maharishi University of Management in Fairfield, Iowa.).

Results from their studies comparing top leaders with average ones in the fields of business, sports and music, showed a clear correlation between mind-brain development and peak performance. These results also indicate that the level of brain integration in world-class athletes is similar to that seen in people who have practised meditation for an average of seven years.

In his book "Invincible Leadership", Dr. Harung states ➔

IT HAS LONG BEEN HYPOTHESISED THAT ACHIEVING ONE'S FULL POTENTIAL IS INTIMATELY RELATED TO DEVELOPING MORE INTEGRATED BRAIN FUNCTIONING.

Dr. Harald Harung

In these studies, brain integration is defined through three brain measures:

- The level of coherence in the different areas of the executive part of the brain.

- Quicker access to the alpha brain waves state (attention to one's inner state of well-being).

- A better match of brain activation and task demands.

In simpler terms, people who have better brain integration have higher emotional stability, decreased anxiety and are more open to new experiences.

According to Harung and Travis, there are three key elements that seem to characterise someone whose brain is powerful and effective:

- The ability to focus on a task, tuning out distractions and interruptions.

- The capacity to adapt in exceptional ways to harness the process of Neuroplasticity (basically the brain changing itself over time).

- The ability to sustain effort over time (meaning never giving up, even when the task may be difficult).

Focusing, adapting and sustaining effort are things that anyone should strive for, even in times when technological distractions are endless.

However, when parts of our brain have been affected by injury or other factors, such as emotional trauma, illness, malnutrition, drugs or alcohol, the brain can lose its balance and start to malfunction. Seeking appropriate and prompt medical advice to fix issues like these can certainly help a person to feel stronger and regain his/her equilibrium.

IT IS ALSO IMPORTANT TO REMEMBER
THAT EVERYONE'S BRAIN IS DIFFERENT
AND LIFE CIRCUMSTANCES ARE UNIQUE
TO EACH PERSON.

HOWEVER, LEARNING ABOUT ONE'S
BRAIN AND IMPROVING THE WAY
IT FUNCTIONS NOT ONLY IS VITAL
BUT IT IS ALSO PERSONAL.
NO ONE CAN DO IT FOR YOU.

BORN OR MADE?

When it comes to leadership, one of the questions that still gets tossed around is 'Are leaders born or made?' Many still believe that leadership is something unattainable and that the learning of certain traits, behaviours or attitudes cannot be done.

In my experience, after years of seeing people learning, growing and developing, this belief cannot be further from the truth. As our brain changes throughout life, our attitudes and behaviours can also change and these include 'leadership behaviours'.

Having said this, it is also true that some people are born with innate leadership abilities, in the same way that others are born with an amazing musical gift. Nonetheless, this doesn't prevent people who are born without these leadership abilities from growing into someone who can lead a project team, start a business or be an inspiration to others by leading a charity campaign. In these examples, those who are willing to have a go and not shy away from leadership may realise that they can influence people and achieve an outcome if they are willing to learn and polish the skills they need to do this successfully.

David A. Waldman, a management professor at Arizona State University, has been investigating if leaders have distinctive brains. Using a qEEG machine, Waldman was able to map out the electrical activity of the brains of senior managers and successful entrepreneurs rated as "inspirational" by their employees.

Part of his conclusion was that these leaders showed higher levels of coherence in the right frontal part of the brain – the area that provides us with the social skills we need to interact well with others.

Waldman believes that it is possible to teach this part of the brain to operate more effectively through the use of neuro-feedback training – a well-known technique that has been used to improve autism, depression, ADD and other ailments for several decades now.

Waldman and his team are endeavouring to unravel how this technique can be implemented to assist the average person to hone in on his or her leadership abilities by enhancing their brain functioning.

HAVE WE FORGOTTEN THE BODY?

Now more than ever, the world of work favours outputs that emerge from the activity of the brain, as thinking and ideas are at the centre of economic enterprises.

Any other process that has to do with what happens inside the rest of our body - for example how our heart 'feels' about a decision, what we know instinctively through our gut or how our cells respond to different stimuli – has been outside what most people consider formal, respectable or logical, particularly when it comes to business interactions. On occasion, it feels to me as if people believe that business transactions just happen without a human being driving them. This causes a void or disconnection that many experience when working, particularly for big organisations.

In the last decade, what we know about our brains and bodies has taken extraordinary leaps, with an increasing number of neuroscientists, pharmacologists and other professionals from the healing world talking about the intelligence of our mind-body. One such person was the late American neuroscientist Dr. Candace Pert.

Dr. Pert discovered the opiate receptor – the cellular binding site for endorphins in the brain and was also the author of more than 250 research papers and the book "Molecules of Emotions". Having become well-known after appearing in the movie "What The Bleep Do We Know?", Dr. Pert pioneered new thinking in regards to the mind and body being entities that are highly connected by molecules which engage in constant cross talk. For example, the communication between the nervous and immune system, of which Dr. Pert said,

"The feelings we have are really chemicals that can help or hurt us."

As I write this chapter, the current news that Australian former Olympic swimming champion, Ian Thorpe, is battling depression makes me think. Having someone of this calibre admitting to it publicly is not only brave but also valuable, as it encourages many others who could be dealing with this debilitating condition to be more proactive.

It is easy for me to relate to what is happening to Thorpe as depression entered my life in 2008. I was able to overcome it by accessing my willpower and with the help of therapy and other methods, but on the way I gained deep insight into mind-body connection and disconnection.

At the time, I devoured Dr. Pert's book and read everything I could get my hands on to understand it and get rid of it. However, perhaps the biggest thing I realised was that it didn't matter how conscious or aware I was of what was happening to me, or how hard I tried to realign my thoughts with the techniques I was learning, the feelings in my body were another matter altogether.

Being someone who reads, researches and is always looking for answers, everything I put in place kicked off the process towards recovery. Still, it did not make much difference to my state of being.

I felt weak and powerless, with my muscles being so feeble and lacking any impulse to get out of bed each morning – it was something incomprehensible to me.

It was in those moments that I understood what Dr. Pert had said about how the chemicals in our brain-body system can potentially hurt us if we do not do anything to change them. I felt lucky to be someone who does not give up easily until I find the solution to a problem. I often think of those who may be suffering from depression or another mental illness and do not have the means, the knowledge or the right people around to help them.

This was a dark period of my life, which I of course would have preferred not to encounter. The positive thing about this experience is that I am now in a position to talk about it first hand, and empathise with others while effortlessly accepting that the body and the mind operate as an integrated whole with the power to affect who we are, how we feel and how we act.

The World Health Organisation estimates that about 121 million people worldwide suffer from depression, with a staggering two-thirds of them not seeking medical assistance. Many go to work and suffer in silence. They do not complain, they do not tell anyone... but the illness is there. As a leader, being prepared to support someone in such circumstances is being 'humane', because you never know, maybe one day, it could happen to you or to someone you love.

The point of this section is to remind us that we operate as a whole unit, a system. Even though cultivating our intelligence or IQ is important to get us through life, it is not the only thing that matters. There are other organs that make up who we are and complex interactions happening between our head brain and the rest of our body; and if they are misaligned, they can affect the way we feel and respond to situations.

~

121 MILLION PEOPLE
SUFFER FROM
DEPRESSION AND
2/3 DO NOT SEEK
MEDICAL ASSISTANCE.

Source: World Health Organisation

THE THREE BRAINS

Dr. Robert Cooper, chairman of the US-based Advanced Excellence Systems wrote in one of his papers: "The dinosaurs of the future will be those who keep trying to live and work from their heads alone. Human brilliance, commitment and creativity may be driven far less by the brain in the head, than by newly discovered intelligence centres – now called 'brain two and brain three' – in the gut and in the heart."

Personally, I have always been more intuitive than analytical. In my professional career, being an intuitive person working with task-oriented managers who considered that the term "trust me" had no relevance when a decision had to be made, was not easy and always left me puzzled and disheartened.

Well-renowned personalities such as Dr. Deepak Chopra – an Indian-American author, holistic health guru and alternative medicine practitioner, American author Malcolm Gladwell, English biologist Rupert Sheldrake and many others have been talking about the power of intuition in recent years, with each attempting to teach others how to use it to their advantage.

I am certain that people in the business world secretly seek the help of professional intuition advisors on how to invest their money or make decisions in business and in life.

But the nature of humans never ceases to surprise me, with many unwilling to openly admit their desire to explore beyond what can be seen or proven, simply because they do not want to be judged by their business colleagues.

Now that neuroscience is providing the empirical evidence with regards to how our bodies and brains work, the doubts that existed about some of these abilities are starting to fade away, giving birth to a renewed and more holistic way of working and living.

I ALWAYS THOUGHT THAT ONE DAY,
THE WORD 'INTUITION' WOULD
NO LONGER BE A "TABOO WORD"
AND IT SEEMS TO ME THAT
THIS DAY HAS ARRIVED.

COMPASSION, BRAIN & BUSINESS

The concept of integrating the brain cannot be complete without addressing the value of compassion and how important it is to bring this capacity back into our lives; an ability that seems to have been lost or forgotten in many of today's workplaces.

When I was in San Francisco in 2013, I was invited to attend the Wisdom 2.0 Conference. This conference, which is expanding into Europe, has a clear mission: "Exploring living with great awareness, wisdom and compassion". The speakers ranged from people in business such as LinkedIn CEO, Jeff Weiner to other famous names in the "society" and "wisdom" streams, like Arianna Huffington, CEO of the Huffington Post and German author Eckhardt Toelle.

These new types of conferences are enabling different segments of our society to come together with the purpose of reviving basic human abilities like compassion; a testament to the belief that we consider them as important qualities, essential for better living.

In my view, the incessant push to maximise efficiencies and profit, in combination with a mechanistic view of humans as existing only to produce an output that benefits a few, has generated discontent and diminished the time that people are able to allocate to connect with one another, to pay attention to each other's needs and to show empathy and compassion.

If it is true that people who are more agreeable are less likely to be promoted and receive less remuneration than the more aggressive type of personalities, then the time has come for recruiters to re-think who they should be recruiting if they are to create a more balanced workforce.

In my view, leaders who want to be effective but lack self-awareness tend to recruit people who are similar to them because it is just easier. Unless told otherwise through direct feedback or by doing a 360-degree assessment, people keep repeating behavioural patterns that may not bring out the best in others, and generally, most of them will not realise the impact they have on the productivity and engagement levels of their staff. Leaders who focus solely on achieving stretch targets and have 'only about the task' meetings, while postponing or cancelling the 'one-on-one' conversations due to lack of time or interest, need to reflect if they really want to take up a more formal leadership role.

A person whose interest is predominantly about how much money can be made and who chooses to devote limited attention to serving others will, without a doubt, be limiting his/ her capacity to influence and lead more effectively. Compassion matters. It creates better leadership, but it can easily disappear as soon as leaders don't place any value on it or don't endeavour to practice it frequently with those around them.

THERE ARE ONLY TWO WAYS TO LIVE YOUR LIFE. ONE IS AS THOUGH NOTHING IS A MIRACLE. THE OTHER IS AS THOUGH EVERYTHING IS A MIRACLE.

Albert Einstein

STRATEGIES TO ENHANCE BRAIN INTEGRATION

There are many strategies that can be used to improve brain integration. Below are some of the ones I believe can make the most difference in anyone's life:

1. DEVELOP YOUR SELF-AWARENESS

Self-reflection:
Take 5 to 10 minutes at the end of the day to reflect in solitude about the thoughts, feelings and reactions you had during the day. Doing this helps you develop a more detached and less subjective or biased perspective about how you respond to the events in your life.

Participate in a 360-degree assessment process:
This type of assessment gives you insights into the behaviours and attitudes you may show to others without realising that you have them (blind spots). This process is an effective starting point in the process of personal transformation.

Seek feedback from the people close to you:
Informally seek feedback from the people who work with you to keep yourself (and your brain) on track particularly when you want to monitor the changes you want to undertake in your life.

2. EVALUATE HOW YOUR BRAIN IS FUNCTIONING

Taking the time to find out if there are any issues that are affecting your brain's performance is an invaluable first step to correct behaviours that may cause you trouble or that you find hard to change.

3. VISIT A NEURO-FEEDBACK SPECIALIST OR NEURO-COACH

Engaging a brain coach will become as common in the future as seeking the guidance of a fitness trainer is today. A properly qualified Neuro-coach can help you devise the most effective strategies to optimise your brain and regulate stress levels.

4. WATCH THE "REDESIGN MY BRAIN" TV SERIES

This Australian 2013 three-part series is a fascinating and fun documentary in which television personality Todd Sampson, undergoes a brain makeover to reverse mental ageing – based on the growing science of brain plasticity. http://www.abc.net.au/tv/programs/redesign-my-brain-with-todd-sampson/

5. JOIN A MINDFULNESS MEDITATION PROGRAM

Deep breathing and the practice of mindful meditation are probably the most effective and the easiest strategies to improve mental function and to reduce negative moods, anxiety and depression.

6. CHALLENGE YOUR BRAIN

Reading books, acquiring new knowledge, learning new skills and participating in activities that are outside your comfort zone help to create new neural connections and allow you to explore your brain's potential.

7. SELF-REGULATE

Learn how to regulate your emotions by taking time for yourself, talking to a therapist or attending an emotional intelligence program. There is always room for improvement when it comes to how we react to the challenges and situations in our lives.

Chapter Eight

INSPIRATION

WHEN WAS THE LAST TIME YOU FELT REALLY INSPIRED?

CAN YOU REMEMBER THAT FEELING?
HOW WOULD YOU DESCRIBE IT?

WHAT IS INSPIRATION, REALLY?

Being inspired can be described as being captivated, entranced or engulfed by a feeling of positive energy drawing you towards a goal or task. When you are inspired, you feel good, energised, motivated and alive.

We all experience inspiration in different ways, to varying degrees and for a number of reasons. Some people are inspired by nature others by in-depth conversations or by learning something new and others by a new goal or project, music, the arts, or sports.

When you are inspired, you are stimulating your mind, especially when you are being creative. This is similar to the feeling of being on a 'high' or perhaps you have heard the expression 'being on cloud nine'.

When you are inspired you want to share the idea with others. Inspiration is often experienced as a feeling of transcendence, a moment of clarity and an awareness of new possibilities beyond the known and the familiar. This enthuses the people around you and it becomes a powerful source that invites others to participate, to follow, to collaborate. In organisations and in life in general, most people will naturally respond and relate to an inspirational leader.

The word inspiration is derived from the Latin word *inspiratus* or *inspirare* and it is fair to think of inspiration as being 'in-spirited', that is, being in the spirit. So it's not a surprise that when you feel inspired, you also experience a sense of enthusiasm.

Interestingly, the word enthusiasm has its origin in the Latin word *entheos* meaning 'in God'. How you interpret God or spirit in this context depends on your personal beliefs and this doesn't have to have any religious connotations.

Being 'in God' or 'inspirited' could also be viewed as your higher intelligence; that is, having a sense of something different or greater than your everyday logical functioning.

Personally, I consider inspiration to be 'the language of your psyche'. The term *psyche* comes from the Greek, meaning 'soul, mind or spirit'. From this, one could say that inspiration is both an insight and an expression of your personal spirit, your essence; not necessarily in a religious sense, but that which makes 'you' uniquely you.

It is also interesting to note that the ancient Greeks actually believed that being inspired was to be in a state of temporary madness — perhaps this is not so crazy after all...

Inspiration is a powerful force that helps ideas, projects and goals come to fruition when acted upon. It is so potent that not only can it make things happen, but also influence others and trigger their enthusiasm. One could say that inspiration is infectious.

TYPES OF INSPIRATION

There are three basic types of inspiration, all of which interrelate to a certain extent. However, it is important to understand how each of the different types work, so you can incorporate and utilise them to their full potential in your life.

The three types are:

- Spontaneous

- Active

- Transactional

SPONTANEOUS INSPIRATION

Spontaneous inspiration is an internal process in which insights emerge naturally or spontaneously and are not necessarily the result of external stimuli.

I am sure you have heard the expression 'a flash of inspiration.' Despite the far-fetched nature of this phrase, if you think about it as chemicals in your brain making their way through your neural pathways, it actually makes a lot of sense. The release of these feel-good chemicals can be quite addictive, which is why many people feel stimulated by the process; and this is also why the term spontaneous inspiration, like spontaneous combustion, is quite descriptive of the actual brain process.

Ideas or problems that spark spontaneous inspiration can be as simple as reading or writing a song or a poem, or coming up with a new business idea. Interestingly, some of the greatest songs of all times were born from a flash of inspiration and written in a very short space of time.

For some people, the more difficult the challenge is to resolve and the more effort exerted, the more powerful the feeling of reward can be. While others might not always understand this, those who stubbornly persevere until they find a way to invent, create or solve something, do so, because when perseverance pays off, the reward is sweet. Thus, we could consider anything that is internally or self-generated to be spontaneous inspiration.

Generally, spontaneous inspiration cannot occur if it doesn't engage or connect with something that is important to you, your essence, spirit or something you truly value. It is an inside-out process, meaning that while inspiration is the result of an internal action, it has an external reaction. For things to come to fruition, you need to act on them.

Spontaneous Inspiration can be blocked by:

- Trying to force it – the more you try to force inspiration, the less inspired you will be.

- Believing that inspiration is something reserved for 'special' people.

- Believing that in order to be inspired, you need to think of an entirely unique idea, something that has not been created or thought of previously.

How to stimulate Spontaneous Inspiration

It is difficult to deliberately stimulate spontaneous inspiration, as it often seems to come out of nowhere. A songwriter will remark, "that song just popped into my head, I don't know where it came from." This sort of inspiration is a synthesis of unconsciously stored information, experiences and creative imagination.

While spontaneous inspiration can happen at any time, we know that for inspiration to emerge, it needs an opportunity to do so. It is harder for flashes of inspiration to emerge when the mind is fully occupied, as it appears through the spaces or gaps in between daily activity and moments of relaxation.

Have you ever had an insight or thought of a possible solution to a problem while taking a shower, lying in bed or sitting quietly in a chair?

The reason for this is the result of your thinking slowing down and creating a gap, which gives inspiration a chance to emerge, like the sun shining through a thick layer of clouds.

So while you can't force spontaneous inspiration, you certainly can give it a chance by quietening your busy mind so the brain can work its magic.

ACTIVE INSPIRATION

Active inspiration refers to being inspired by external elements that stimulate you into action; for example, when you listen to an inspirational speech, delve into the biography of a person you admire or read moving quotes.

SEE IT

Observing others who are experts in their field is one of the major sources of inspiration that encourages young people to take a certain career path. Those who make major achievements in their area of expertise often attribute their inspiration to someone who has been a role model to them.

HEAR IT

Sometimes a favourite piece of music you love can inspire you. Athletes, such as Australian Lleyton Hewitt, frequently use this method. The former No. 1 tennis player in the world, Hewitt is renowned for listening to the theme from the movie *Rocky* before his matches.

MOVE IT

Exercising is another great tool that can help you be inspired as feel-good chemicals called endorphins get released when we exercise. Any external factor that helps trigger your inspiration resulting in motivation is 'active inspiration'.

How to stimulate Active Inspiration

- Read, watch or listen to something that inspires you. There are many great biographies and other inspirational books, videos and programs that can spark your inspiration.

- Play your favourite piece of music before giving a talk, doing a presentation, or at any other time when you want to feel inspired.

- Keep the company of people who are encouraging and uplifting.

- Have photos or images around which can make you feel good.

TRANSACTIONAL INSPIRATION

Whereas with active inspiration you are inspired by external influences, transactional inspiration occurs when you develop the ability to inspire others.

The closer your values and interests are aligned, the easier it will be to transfer and ignite inspiration in others. As an example, Steve Jobs' inspiration worked by combining existing elements together in new ways. By first inspiring himself, he was able to inspire those around him, and then the rest of the world!

While one may not do anything as far-reaching as what Jobs created, transactional inspiration is essential for being a great leader, as you want to engage, encourage and motivate others to 'come on board' and embrace your vision.

As mentioned, inspiration is contagious, even more so than enthusiasm. While you might be enthusiastic about something, it doesn't mean that it will inspire others, especially if their values and interests don't match yours. You might be enthusiastic about a certain project that someone else has absolutely no interest in. If this mismatch happens regularly in a team you are leading or working with, you may need to assess the composition of the team.

In order for inspiration to be contagious, there needs to be a common value or interest, a common cause or goal, or a perceived personal benefit. Leaders who are championing a cause find it easier to inspire others. Just think about the famous "I have a dream" speech by Martin Luther King, Jr. He was certainly an inspiring and visionary leader.

HOW TO STIMULATE TRANSACTIONAL INSPIRATION

While there is no standard recipe, below are some general principles that may help you inspire others:

- The more an idea connects with people's values and interests, the more they will be emotionally engaged. Remember that emotional engagement – feeling good about something – is the key to motivation. Make sure that besides any logical argument or reasoning, you appeal to people's values.

- The more sincere, genuine, authentic and ethical you are, the more people will trust you and follow you.

- Focus on the idea, solution or opportunity rather than the problem.

- Address the 'why factor', that is, the purpose. Why should 'we' be doing this?

- Facilitate insight. Rather than doing a 'sales job' by trying to convince people, it is better for them to make the connection themselves as to why something might be important or exciting.

- Understand what makes people tick by developing your listening and emotional intelligence skills.

- It seems that the 'carrot' inspires people more than the 'stick'. While a stick might get people to comply, it certainly doesn't engage, let alone inspire and motivate. At its core, the human brain is like most other organisms – it retreats and protects itself when there is real or perceived danger and it moves towards a reward if the circumstances are favourable. Encouragement, engagement and positive feedback happen more easily when you want to inspire people. As a leader, you want people to come along with you and not retreat away from you. You will sometimes hear people say – 'I am successful because someone believed in me and I felt inspired to keep moving forward.'

WHY BOTHER WITH INSPIRATION?

Nearly every human being will have many ideas that can inspire others during his or her lifetime, but it is a sad fact that many people never really act on any of them.

Remember that inspiration is often the result of something that you value or something that is important to you; and what inspires you gives an insight into the essence of who you are and what makes you tick.

I do believe that if you fail to act on inspiration and ignore good ideas, eventually your brain switches this ability off – as if to say why bother? This doesn't mean you should blindly follow your flashes of inspiration without being discerning and doing your due diligence.

INSPIRATION – DIVINE OR INGENIOUS?

So perhaps inspiration has not so much to do with divinity but with ingenuity; when you become more aware and start paying attention to when you feel inspired, regardless of the extent, you will certainly add another dimension to your life.

You will be surprised how many more ideas start to flow. After all, inspiration means to be 'in-spirited' (being in the spirit). When you are in-spirited, you feel more alive and you can truly express yourself.

Inspiration is just the beginning of the story, it is like a flame that ignites so things can start happening. While it is great to feel the initial rush of feel-good chemicals, this soon diminishes; and if you don't follow up on your inspiration, it is likely to lead to a sense of frustration.

This is especially the case if you have a history of not finishing what you started. But even that has a time limit, as frustration, dissatisfaction and feeling discontented eventually turns into giving up, experiencing apathy, or perhaps even depression.

As mentioned previously, while it is important not to indiscriminately act upon your inspiration, when you do act, many things will come to fruition. Here is often where the hard work starts. This is the point where, for many, the original flash of inspiration ends pretty quickly, as they don't want to do what it takes for the inspiration, the insights or the ideas to see the light of day. But those who do persevere get to see and experience the fruits of their labour.

For most readers, relating to and accepting the concept of inspiration will be relatively easy. Without hesitation you may say, 'that really was an inspirational speaker' whilst not knowing precisely how or why they were inspiring to you!

In this context, you understand what inspiration means as you may have experienced being inspired before. So ask yourself, how can I be a more inspirational leader and what would the specific benefits be for me and for others, if I were more inspirational?

INSPIRATION IS FICKLE

While inspiration can be harnessed, it ultimately knows no hard and fast rules and can be quite fickle.

Sometimes when you need it the most, it remains silent, while at other times it just appears from nowhere. Thomas Edison was partly right when he said ⊕

"Genius is 1% inspiration and 99% perspiration."

Keep in mind that some of the most popular songs were written in less than half an hour; but they still had to be written down, recorded, produced, marketed and played in order for you to hear them.

So whatever inspires you, wherever your inspiration comes from and however you inspire others, remember that inspiration is a powerful force...

And may that force be with you.

IF YOU TREAT AN INDIVIDUAL AS HE IS, HE WILL REMAIN HOW HE IS. BUT IF YOU TREAT HIM AS IF HE WERE WHAT HE OUGHT TO BE AND COULD BE, HE WILL BECOME WHAT HE OUGHT TO BE AND COULD BE.

Johann Wolfgang von Goethe

Chapter Nine

IMAGINATION

IMAGINE A WORLD WITHOUT IMAGINATION. SERIOUSLY.

TAKE A MOMENT AND IMAGINE HOW DIFFERENT OUR WORLD WOULD BE WITHOUT THE POWERFUL BRAIN ABILITY CALLED IMAGINATION.

THE POWERFUL WORLD OF UNLIMITED POSSIBILITIES

In our everyday world, almost every item we see is the result of human imagination. Unlike any other living creature on this planet, we have the extraordinary ability not to only reason but also to imagine, dream, fantasise and create images in our minds.

Yet, when we talk about using our imagination, it somehow becomes a vague concept, a skill limited to the crazy, eccentric people; to the artists, inventors, musicians, composers, writers, choreographers and architects. We tend to mystify imagination as if some have it and others don't. While it is true that some people find it easier to imagine or visualise than others, often without being consciously aware of doing so, every functioning human being imagines in nearly every waking moment – even when we are asleep, as we dream.

We can imagine, fantasise and visualise all kinds of things beyond current reality, boundaries and limitations. Indeed, the word 'imagination' comes from the Latin *imaginatio*, a synonym for *phantasia*, from which our modern word 'fantasy' derives.

People we consider geniuses like Leonardo Da Vinci, Albert Einstein, Michelangelo, Thomas Jefferson, William Shakespeare, Mozart and in our time Bill Gates and Steven Spielberg to name a few, would never have been heard of without the ability to use this higher intelligence called imagination. The mind's faculty to imagine has changed and will continue to change our world despite many people taking it for granted and not utilising it as much as they could.

It is now known that using imagination generates new associations in the brain which can lead to creative insights. This alone is positively amazing, but imagination also has the ability to change your behaviour, improve your performance and heal your body. The most exquisite art, literature, music and scientific advancements are the result of this extraordinary brain activity.

IMAGINATION - THE LANGUAGE OF YOUR ESSENCE

Imagination is considered by many psychologists as the language of our essence and in a way, it is a unique expression of one's mind and spirit.

Imagination, hopes, dreams and fantasies give a lot of insight into who we are, who we want to be and how we want to live our lives.

When you don't allow yourself to be informed by this 'soul' language, let alone integrate it in a functional way, you will somehow feel incomplete. Your essence wants to express itself and your imagination gives you many clues and guidance as to how this can be achieved.

IMAGINATION AND BRAIN FUNCTIONING

The ability of human beings to visualise and imagine things is truly remarkable. The brain processes involved in imagination, however, have been quite unknown until now.

A new study from researcher Alex Schlegel from Dartmouth College's Department of Psychology and Brain Science, found that the activity we call imagination is the product of a widespread network of neurons (the scientists call it the "mental workspace") that consciously alters and manipulates images, symbols and ideas, providing the intense mental focus needed to come up with new ideas and solutions to complex problems.

What we are able to imagine is the result of the interaction between all these networks in the brain and it is certainly a powerful process. For example, we know that when you activate the visual cortex (at the back of your head) through imagination, you also activate your senses, feelings and emotions, as well as other parts of your physical body.

If you imagine your favourite song right now, you can actually recreate the sound in your head, hear it and sing along. If you visualise throwing a ball, tiny electrical impulses in the muscles of your arm are activated and react as if you were actually doing it.

When you imagine sucking a sour lemon or think about eating food that repulses you, it is most likely that you will experience a reaction, such as your salivary glands activating or your face changing into a look of displeasure.

LANGUAGE IS VISUAL

Our unique human ability to communicate and share ideas would not be possible without our ability to imagine things.

How do you know what the words cloud, elephant or rose mean? Trying to say these words without the associated images coming up is near impossible (just try it).

The way we are introduced to language, often starts when a parent points at himself/herself and says 'Daddy/Mummy' and it is often the first word a child will say, much to the delight of the parent. The same principle applies when the parent points at a physical image of a cloud, elephant or rose and repeats the word several times, until the child does the same.

Nearly all language is learnt in a visual context and we often learn a new word by using that word in a sentence to represent an image or describe a scenario.

A great example of this is the beautiful scene from the movie of the novel "The Book Thief" (2013). The protagonist, Liesel Meminger, is describing to her friend Max, the young Jewish man who is hiding under the house, what the weather looks like.

He asks her to use words that could help him picture what is happening outside the house.

After stumbling with a few words, similar to the ones most people would use to describe the sun, Liesel then uses the expression "the sun looks like a silver oyster."

He smiles at her and with his finger pointing at his head, he says: ⊕

"Thank you, I got that now'".

THE POWER OF IMAGINATION

While most people use their imagination mainly subconsciously, there are many practical ways to use it with conscious awareness.

You can harness the power of the imagination and make it work for you. To do this, it is important to define imagination beyond its concept. We could classify imagination into the following nine types:

1. *Factual imagination*

   Imagining and visualising things that already exist.

2. *Functional imagination*

   Using imagination and visualisation for mental rehearsal – to make a change or improvement.

3. *Creative imagination*

   Making up new things that might contain aspects of what already exists and creating new combinations and possibilities including solutions and innovation.

4. *Active imagination*

   Using imagery to access the unconscious mind to uncover information, often from the past.

5. *Guided imagination*

   Using imagery as a technique to influence the subconscious mind.

6. *Fictional imagination*

   Making things up that are highly improbable.

7. *Reactive imagination*

   Imagery based on impulses.

8. *Empathic imagination*

   Visualising what something might feel like for another person.

9. *Destructive imagination*

   Using imagination to destroy rather than to create.

EXPLORING THE TYPES OF IMAGINATION ➜

FACTUAL IMAGINATION

Factual imagination is visualising objects, people or things that are already known to you, like visualising your car, your house or your workplace.

It may also involve visualising yourself in other locations, like your favourite holiday destination or sitting on your couch at home.

If you couldn't visualise what your car looks like, it would be difficult to remember where you parked it. Factual imagination can help you with strategising and planning for a relaxing weekend. You can use factual imagination to envision what your living room could look like if you changed the furniture around or how a chair you are about to purchase would fit in a specific room.

You can also utilise factual imagination when you are feeling stressed and want to shift your brain into a 'different gear' to help you slow down and clarify your thinking. By imagining yourself in your favourite place, you can shift your brain to a more relaxed state.

FUNCTIONAL IMAGINATION

Functional imagination is used to 'reprogram' your brain through visualising a new desired behaviour or to develop new skills, beliefs and attitudes.

Functional imagination can reinforce and create new neural pathways so that the imagined actions, behaviours or beliefs can become a reality.

If you repeatedly imagine yourself being confident, capable and successful, you will develop the specific neural pathways that will make you feel more confident, capable and successful.

Top athletes use functional imagination as an important part of their mental training and preparation. For example, mentally practicing a perfect golf swing, a backhand in tennis or repeating your shooting motion in basketball, actually improves that particular skill. You can do things perfectly in your mind again and again to develop these neural pathways.

You can imagine yourself giving a great presentation or doing well in a job interview while seeing yourself calm, relaxed and confident before you actually do it. As far as your subconscious mind is concerned, by the time the event occurs in real life, you have already done it a number of times and you won't be so tense.

This is also why the expressions 'fake it till you make it' and 'acting as if' are actually not as silly as they may sound. Successful people imagine themselves being successful, even when sometimes there are plenty of reasons to doubt it. Hence, the advice to hang on to your vision.

Top athletes devote part of their actual physical training to training themselves mentally. Remember that in general, actions will follow what you envision. Athletes never imagine themselves losing the big game; in their minds, they are always victorious.

Of course, the same principle applies if you focus on the negative instead of the positive. As a matter of fact, most people use functional imagination to hinder rather than to help themselves. Instead of visualising what they want, they imagine what they don't want, reinforcing the image with statements like, "I don't feel very confident", "I am not very good at that", etc.

CREATIVE IMAGINATION

Creative imagination is used for creating, inventing or problem solving. While certain components may already exist, you create something new by putting them together in a different order.

Part of creative imagination is the ability to combine mental images and concepts to form new ideas. A comedian, a story teller, an author or an artist all have creative and vivid imaginations, where often existing components are combined in a novel and creative way. Creative imagination is not, however, limited to inventors, artists and designers. It can just as easily be applied to a practical purpose such as a scientific discovery.

Developing creative thinking involves being able to entertain hypotheticals, dream, make things up and take risks. The creative part of the brain is usually stimulated by hypothetical 'what if' questions.

To activate your creative thinking, you need to entertain opportunity and possibility-type questions such as: "Imagine that…"; "What would it look like if…"; "How would we go about…"

A great way to stimulate creative imagination is to start with the end in mind, seeing the finished result and then working backwards. By doing this, you will activate your brain to look for the solutions you need. Imagination opens up your brain to the world of possibilities beyond real or perceived limitations.

WE ARE WHAT WE IMAGINE OURSELVES TO BE.

Kurt Vonnegut

There are two things that usually stand in the way when trying to use creative imagination:

- Your belief and attitude, thinking that something cannot be done.

- Problem orientation, where the focus is on the obstacles.

These are the biggest hurdles for most people to overcome. What you need to develop to encourage and enhance creative imagination is to become possibility orientated, where the focus is on solutions rather than on why something will not work. You want to move away from the idea of "it can't be done" to "how can it be done?" Those who consider themselves pragmatic, practical, logical and fact-driven often find creative thinking quite challenging.

These types of people find security and comfort in what is known rather than daring to dream of what might be possible, as this makes them feel insecure.

Too often, people consider the challenges of the situation first, as well as every reason why it can't be done. Rather than reaching a new destination, they fall over at the first hurdle and go back to what is more familiar. To enhance your creative imagination, you need to teach your brain the 'upside down principle' of starting with the end in mind and then working your way backwards. This is no different than an architect designing a building, then working backwards to focus on the building plans before the actual work commences.

ACTIVE IMAGINATION

Active imagination is used in coaching, counselling and in psychotherapeutic settings. It is often used to facilitate a healing or development process.

Active imagination is a methodology that activates the information that gets stored in the unconscious mind. Thought patterns, desires, deep-seated beliefs and values can lie below the level of awareness, not easily accessible to the conscious mind. These unconscious thought patterns or beliefs are often based on childhood experiences that include repressed memories, which can drive and control our actions.

Because imagination is a whole brain process, it is very effective in bringing unconscious information to the surface, which helps us to understand what has been driving someone's behaviours, thoughts and actions.

Bringing information into conscious awareness through the process of active imagination is very useful for broadening your options and decision making. Active imagination is also effective in imagining future scenarios, as if the change towards an ideal situation had already occurred.

As we have already seen when describing functional imagination, this not only helps the brain open up to new possibilities, but it can also move you beyond current perceived limitations.

GUIDED IMAGINATION

Guided imagination is using imagery as a tool to influence the subconscious mind. Guided imagination encompasses a variety of techniques.

These techniques include visualisation, the use of images, metaphors, symbols, drawing and storytelling. It is often used in hypnotherapy for the purpose of influencing the subconscious to change behaviour, help to increase performance or make behavioural changes such as giving up smoking or losing weight.

Guided imagination is also used to relieve symptoms of pain, depression and anxiety. In addition, it can help to boost the body's immune system. The power of imagination and the effect it has on the body are quite remarkable. As with active imagination, guided imagination is often facilitated by someone like a health practitioner, clinical hypnotherapist or experienced coach.

FICTIONAL IMAGINATION

Fictional imagination is the mind's ability to make up things which have no basis in fact or reality.

It is imagining things that do not or are highly unlikely to exist – things that are 'way out there'. There can be functional aspects of fictional imagination, particularly for creative artists such as authors, screenwriters, sculptors and painters; for example imagining situations and worlds that do not exist, which are often used to write books, movies and TV series scripts.

While this type of fictional imagination is considered functional, there is also a dysfunctional imagination that includes hallucinations or delusions, common in mental illnesses (schizophrenia, bi-polar disorder, etc.).

REACTIVE IMAGINATION

Reactive imagination is based on strong emotions such as excessive fear or optimism.

It generally means imagining the best or worst possible outcomes. The reason it is called reactive imagination is because it is often impulse driven. For example, you might have some undefined symptoms of illness that are not easy to diagnose and you start to imagine having an incurable disease.

Or when someone you love comes home unusually late at night, you may fear they are engaged in some sort of illicit behaviour. Those who have suffered from jealousy know that reactive imagination can take over one's mind.

Reactive imagination is especially problematic in our relationships with others. It is important to apply impulse control to reactive imagination.

EMPATHIC IMAGINATION

Empathic imagination is the basis of both compassion and empathy and it is essential in developing social skills.

Empathic imagination is at the core of emotional intelligence, as you are able to imagine and connect to what another person might be feeling and experiencing. In this case, you activate the mirror neuron system in your brain that fires as the result of observing emotions and intention in others.

These mirror neurons trigger functions in your brain which activate similar emotions within you. For example, when you witness someone being sad and distressed, you too can experience and connect with sadness to some extent. Just think of a movie that has deeply touched you when all you were doing was watching images on a screen.

Empathic imagination also enables you to create an understanding of people who have different objectives, values and knowledge, by envisaging the world from that person's point of view. This gives us the ability to 'walk in their shoes'. It doesn't necessarily mean you have to have had a similar experience. It doesn't mean agreeing with that person's point of view, but it certainly will result in decreasing judgment and increasing tolerance, which is likely to promote problem solving through collaboration and cooperation.

Empathic imagination not only helps you to understand and connect with others, but it is also a fundamental element in engaging and motivating others. Based on the mirror neuron principle, when people feel you are empathetic and understanding towards them, they feel safe in your presence, rather than threatened.

The old style of leadership, using the stick approach rather than empathy, was thought to motivate people. Unfortunately, there are still managers and leaders who obstinately believe the stick approach works best.

DESTRUCTIVE IMAGINATION

Destructive imagination is the dark side of imagination, the opposite or the 'shadow side' of creative imagination.

It is the ability to envisage and form new ideas that can be used for destruction such as planning to take revenge on someone or wanting to ruin something.

Destructive imagination has given birth to some of the most horrendous crimes in human history like the Holocaust, the planned and systematic mass killing by Adolf Hitler in Nazi Germany. Whilst that act was at the extreme far end of the scale, nearly all functional human beings may engage in some destructive imagination at some stage in their lives.

Understanding the different types of imagination will help you recognise them and use imagination more deliberately, purposefully and effectively. You can be more in control and know when imagination can serve you or hinder you.

IMAGINATION: A LEADER'S BEST FRIEND

One secret ingredient that nearly all successful people share is how to use imagination in their favour.

Both Bill Gates and Steve Jobs used their imagination, envisaging how personal computers could change the world, the way we work, how we could educate our children and how we would entertain ourselves. They were certainly right!

HOW TO ENHANCE YOUR IMAGINATION

- **Start with the end in mind**

  As a leader, you firstly need to know your goal and have a vision of what you want to achieve. As previously mentioned, this is the same path you need to take when you build a house. It is important to have a clear vision of what the end result looks like, unless you are happy to just throw materials together and see what happens. It is vital to apply creative imagination as described earlier, especially the upside-down principle.

  While it might sound rather obvious to begin with the end in mind, you would be surprised how many people don't have a clear vision of what they would like to achieve, let alone how to get there. Instead, they are held back from what they want to achieve by focusing on the obstacles that get in the way. You need to have a strong, clear vision and most importantly, know why your vision is so important to you.

- **Apply the creative and empathic imagination**

  Creative imagination together with empathic imagination is a very powerful combination. If you look back at some of the great leaders of the past, most of them had a purpose, something bigger than what they wanted to achieve for themselves.

  Great leaders often have a passion that addresses the plight of other people rather than what they want for themselves. Even if they have experienced hardship, they are able to imagine what it would be like for people in worse conditions. Just think of people like Mahatma Gandhi, Nelson Mandela and Mother Teresa – they were very much driven by their empathic imagination.

○ Engage the imagination of others

It is much easier to discourage than to encourage people's imagination, especially if it is not part of the work culture. Sometimes it might take some courage to go against a restrictive way of thinking. As someone said to me recently, "I'd rather have my idea shot down than not say anything and a lesser idea be put forward."

Edward de Bono's Six Hat Thinking Methodology has been effective and popular in encouraging people in the workplace to activate their imagination. The Red hat represents intuition, feelings and hunches and the Green hat represents creative ideas and possibilities. As a leader of a team, it may be a good idea to read or become trained in the Six Hat Thinking process.

In the business world where reason, reality, facts and pragmatism prevail, I have seen people looking worried and even embarrassed when asked to use their imagination – as if imagining things was something only children or creative people can do.

The belief that imagination is somehow inferior to logical reasoning often kills, stifles or smothers potential. Not only can this belief hinder great ideas but it also shows a lack of understanding about the important role that imagination plays in human life.

THE IMPORTANCE OF IMAGINATION

Imagination plays a bigger role in our life than what most people believe. The ability to imagine things pervades our entire existence. It influences everything we do, think about and create. It leads to elaborate theories, dreams and inventions in any profession from the realms of academia to engineering and the arts. Ultimately, imagination influences everything we do regardless of our profession. Imagination is the key to innovation.

So think for a moment and reflect on how you could use your imagination more effectively and deliberately. How would your life be personally and professionally improved if you were to activate your brain in ways you have not done before? Imagine if you could bring this higher intelligence into your daily conscious awareness. How much more satisfying and enriched would your life be? Just imagine.

There is nothing childish or shameful about making imagination a vital part of your leadership competencies. The more you use your imagination, the stronger your 'imagination muscle' will become. You will be pleasantly surprised as you use this ability and tap into this rich source of infinite possibilities.

Yesterday's knowledge alone will not suffice. Imagination is essential for anyone, especially for leaders, who not only have to lead people into the future but have to foresee the challenges not yet known that await mankind.

THE MAN WHO HAS NO IMAGINATION, HAS NO WINGS.

Muhammad Ali

Chapter Ten

INTUITION

INTUITION IS ALWAYS RIGHT IN AT LEAST TWO IMPORTANT WAYS. IT IS ALWAYS IN RESPONSE TO SOMETHING AND IT ALWAYS HAS YOUR BEST INTEREST AT HEART.

Gavin de Becker

WHAT IS INTUITION?

There always seems to be a lot of confusion around the concept of intuition and even though we use our intuition on a daily basis, people often tend to think of it as being something airy-fairy, mystical or even paranormal.

However, people will say without any hesitation "I knew it, I should have listened to my intuition!"

Intuition is a sense or perception, a faculty, just like your senses of smell, taste, hearing, sight and touch. It helps you obtain information in a way that differs from your logical and rational thinking.

The word intuition comes from the Latin verb *intueri*, meaning 'to look inside'. It can be experienced in different ways and at different times. Sometimes it expresses itself in pictures or symbols. Other times it is something more internal – often described as a 'gut feeling', a sense or a hunch.

I have no doubt that in the years to come, as experts from the field of neuro-gastroenterology continue to study the role of the neurons that exist in the gut new insights into how 'gut feelings' really work will help to clarify our understanding of intuition as a human ability.

So far we know that intuition provides us with information, insights and views perceived outside the realm of conscious cognition. It's important to point out that although women seem to be better at intuition, men also have this ability. Men seem to be more comfortable using the term 'gut feeling' or 'hunch' when referring to it. All functional human beings have intuitive ability and use it daily, sometimes without being consciously aware that this is taking place.

It is likely that some people are more intuitive than others and use intuition more often in their decision making process. Swiss psychologist Carl Jung was one of the first, in the Western world, to suggest that some personality types are more intuitive than others.

PRACTICAL INTUITION

Intuitives such as American author Laura Day explain that a wide variety of professional people use intuition very often in their daily lives and for very practical reasons.

These professionals include: business managers, entrepreneurs, leaders, stock-market traders, artists, academics, athletes, psychologists, doctors, scientists and even those in the legal profession.

One of my friends, who works as an accident and emergency physician, will say that he relies significantly on his intuition at work because there is very limited time to gather all the hard data you need to make a quick decision when everything around occurs in a matter of minutes or even seconds.

Of course, his intuition is based on very solid knowledge and experience; whereas you and I, unless we are trained, would be useless in a situation like that, regardless of how intuitive we are. So it would be fair to say that this type of practical intuition is skill-dependent and based on a memory bank of knowledge, information and experiences, stored in the long-term memory part of the brain.

CAN YOU POINT AT IT?

We know that practical intuition is a sensation stemming from sensory awareness, which provides a kind of knowing that relies upon the capacity to read signals, cues and patterns, and as previously explained, it is often based on the total sum of our accumulated experiences.

While we can enhance this ability through deliberate observation, recent research has identified the brain regions involved in the process of what Dr. Matthew Lieberman, from the University of California, calls 'intuitive social cognition'.

The picture starting to emerge is that intuitive processing is located in a network of structures inside the brain and that these structures exist in both hemispheres, instead of being located in a specific hemisphere.

IS IT RELIABLE?

The information we gain through this way of knowing – this inner knowing – could be unreliable if we mistakenly interpret wishful thinking as intuition.

Gamblers are renowned for betting on their gut instinct, often with disastrous results because wishful thinking is disguising itself as intuition. At the same time, our intuition can be very useful and valuable, as intuition in itself isn't confusing or ambivalent. It is what we do with that information that counts.

So how can you know when to trust your intuition and when not to trust it? The bad news is that you can never be 100% sure as intuition is not something to merely reject or fully trust. The good news is that you can make your intuition work for you more reliably and effectively, and many people do!

If you trust this basic inner knowing as another source of information, you can make it part of the process of conscious deliberation and discernment. You need to treat intuition as another aspect, a valuable ingredient, that can be taken into account. Using intuition in this way can certainly speed up your decision making process and make you more agile.

DECISIONS AREN'T BASED ON PURE LOGIC

Many people will tell you that thinking, deliberation and decision-making are logical and rational processes, but we now know this to be incorrect.

Neuroscientist Antonio Damasio was one of the first to tell the world that without your 'feeling' faculty, you can't make decisions. Damasio came to this conclusion after analysing patients with brain injury in a particular part of the brain called ventromedial prefrontal cortex – located just behind the nose. The interplay between your rational mind, gut feelings, emotions and intuition all play a very important part in making decisions.

When you value these various aspects and allow them to interact, guided by the logical part of your brain, you will engage in better decision-making. Decisions are not mere products of a rational process, they also involve paying attention to your intuition and on occasion, intuition is the only thing you can use, as other types of information may not be available.

Dr. Gerd Gigerenzer, author of the book "Gut Feeling: The Intelligence of the Unconscious" and director of the Center for Adaptive Behaviour and Cognition at the Max Plank Institute in Germany, has analysed intuition and how it is used in business. In an interview, he reveals that when asked the question about how they make important decisions, most CEOs will say that it is with their gut. Despite this, as intuition is not yet accepted as a tool for such matters, a consultant or employee is usually hired to write a report with enough data to back up the decisions that have already been made, costing time and money to the business.

"We live in a society that trusts algorithms more than intuition" says Dr. Gigerenzer, "although we know that numbers can sometimes be wrong".

In his view, the essence of the intuitive process follows simple heuristics: making a decision taking into consideration one important aspect (or piece of information) and ignoring the rest. This has stirred an increasing interest in the research community and a number of studies are being performed to analyse the outcomes of such decisions.

TO ACT OR NOT TO ACT?

So do you act on your intuition or not? Unfortunately, there isn't a clear and direct answer, instruction or script that you can follow; and while intuition is a valuable source of information, it can also be unreliable.

Intuition is influenced by factors such as: your personal experiences, expectations, values and needs. Here are a few things to look out:

- Don't act blindly on your intuition or insight as if it is the gospel.

- Don't ignore or dismiss your intuition either. Just because you can't logically explain something based on a hunch, a sense or feeling – it doesn't mean that it is useless or baseless.

- Don't let your wishful thinking drown out any alarm bells. A typical example of this is the beginning of a new relationship and when you feel something is not quite right, but you hope you are either wrong or that something will change to match your expectations.

LISTEN – ACKNOWLEDGE – CONSIDER

I believe that intuition is more accurate in situations when you hesitate, feel unsure or when something just doesn't feel quite right.

For example – someone might have all the right qualifications and skills for a specific position and everything appears to add up, yet, you feel that something is not right, but you can't quite put your finger on it. Perhaps it is a business deal, starting out in a romantic relationship or engaging a new business associate, when your intuition tells you that all is not as it seems.

It is important not to ignore this discomfort and let your rational mind overrule it. You would certainly be wise to make the information part of your deliberation process. My advice is to listen, acknowledge and consider intuitive insights together with rational and logical information.

It is very common for people to ignore intuitive early warning signals and be left asking 'why?' when a partnership, relationship or project goes wrong. But if you think back to the first three interactions, ask yourself: Were there already early signals and misgivings that you ignored?

You will be surprised how often 'the DNA' of a personal or professional relationship reveals itself in the first three interactions or so. At this stage, your intuition is already many steps ahead of your conscious knowing, so it is always beneficial to consider this intuitive information.

PREDICTION OR INTUITION

While intuition is gaining an insight into a current situation based on a sense, gut feeling or hunch, a prediction relates more to the sense of what might happen, often without any apparent conscious reason for sensing it.

A prediction is a feeling of anticipation, or perhaps forewarning, of something that could happen. Studies conducted in America with the purpose of analysing how it is possible that 4% of the best top gun fighter pilots are able to hit 40% of the targets reveal that certain pilots are better at anticipation than others (who are equally well trained). They are able to successfully sense the future and make quick decisions, even upside-down while travelling at the speed of light.

However, there is a belief that if you can't measure something, then it doesn't exist.

Perhaps a time will come when we can measure and find evidence of exactly where intuition and prediction originate from within the brain and how we can benefit from them.

HOW INTUITION CAN HELP YOU

Intuition is an invaluable ingredient that can serve you in many aspects of your life and can help you become a more agile leader. Besides the automatic intuitive and spontaneous hunches, you can consciously and deliberately enhance your intuition.

These are some of the benefits:

- It enhances your decision-making process.

- It brings new and creative ideas to life that conscious thinking alone could not achieve.

- It allows you to know without thinking so you can adapt to uncertain conditions more rapidly.

- It guides your actions when situations seem ambiguous.

- It provides an insight into your emotions when it comes to assessing how you feel about a person.

- It increases your empathy and sensitivity towards others, enhancing your emotional intelligence – essential for relating successfully.

- It provides clarity when the conscious mind is confused.

HOW TO ENHANCE YOUR INTUITION

○ **Keep an open mind**

Make sure your logical mind and scepticism don't stand in the way of these processes. You can always critique the information afterwards, but don't reject anything prematurely. Keep an open mind – because just like an invited guest, intuition can't come in if you don't open the door.

○ **Meditate to still the mind**

Meditation is considered one of the best strategies to access intuition. The brain works best when you are in a relaxed state. Leaders who have been meditating regularly for several years are considered more intuitive. Meditation calms the mind, helps you to focus on the present (here and now) and allows intuition to flow. Fifteen minutes of meditation per day (first thing in the morning, for example) helps to improve intuition greatly.

○ **Make it work while you are asleep**

When you have to face a challenge you are unsure about, put your intuition to work while you sleep. Posing a question just before you go to bed and without trying to consciously find the answer, let's your brain do the work by putting it into search mode. Don't try to go through all the scenarios just before you go to sleep as you can do that during the waking hours. Make sure you've got a notepad next to your bed in case you get a flash of inspiration during the night. You also might want to take note of your dreams when you wake up in the morning.

○ **Spontaneous writing**

In your waking hours do some creative and spontaneous writing without trying to be grammatically correct or worrying about making sense on an issue that is affecting you. If you are more artistic, you could do a drawing or painting as a medium instead. Even just doodling on a sheet of paper or randomly writing down a combination of words, pictures, feelings and observations taps into different parts of your brain. Try a variety of things to see what works best for you.

○ **Notice the "silent voice"**

Pay more attention to the quiet voice or hunch when you are interacting with other people. Doing this will assist you to become more attuned to the sensations, mostly in the area around the abdomen. Most people know this sensation well, for example, when they feel nervous or anxious prior to giving a speech or sitting in the dentist's waiting room.

If you pride yourself on being a logical, analytical person – become more aware of how you feel and learn to notice the more subtle sensations in your body. Sometimes you may not be able to put your finger on exactly why, what and where you are getting a feeling, that's why people say things like, "I don't know exactly but it just doesn't feel right."

Keep an intuition journal

Note how you intuitively feel about a situation or decision first and then write down the actual outcome or result after it happens. Go back to review how you originally felt. In this way, you will start to notice how accurate or inaccurate your intuition was.

Take your thoughts for a walk

Remember the more stressed you are, the less intuitive you will be. While stress activates instinctual responses, it is not good for accessing your intuition. When you are busy in your waking hours you tend to be in a 'beta brainwave' state. Intuition works better in an 'alpha brainwave' state, that is, when the electricity between the cells inside your brain are travelling at a lower speed.

This happens when you are awake but relaxed. In this state, you have access to different parts of the brain where creativity and inspiration come from. That is why it's good to take your 'thoughts for a walk', meaning take some time out to walk, in nature if possible, or do some light exercise, as this will spark your intuition.

INTUITION: AN ADVISOR ON YOUR TEAM

Intuition is a great resource to have in your leadership tool box. It is becoming increasingly important that people in the business world are able to make quicker decisions to match the requirements of this fast-paced world.

Examples of business leaders who use intuition are Oprah Winfrey, Richard Branson and George Soros. Oprah, for example, recognises in many of her writings that her intuition has been a major asset in her life.

It is up to you as to how you use intuition as a tool. Remember that intuition is information. Use it just like another 'advisor on your team' who provides you with a different perspective.

Clearly, there are limitations to making intuitive decisions. However, the more research and discussions that are undertaken to understand the brain and body processes that underpin intuitive decision making, the more this faculty will become a more accepted element of management and organisational practices.

In a world where evidence, facts and reason have been considered superior and more valuable than an idea that appears less tangible, it is understandable that many people seem somewhat less comfortable with the concept of intuition. As we have seen previously, whilst perhaps we are not always consciously aware, we use our intuition daily. Intuition plays an integral part in our sense of 'knowing'. Remember that one of intuition's main functions is survival, the sense of knowing when something is amiss or different, therefore determining if you are in danger or not; a primary function that is shared with other primates.

Many effective leaders rely heavily on their intuition, with the vast majority of people unaware that the bulk of their decisions are purely based on a mix of emotions and intuitive hunches; and while not attributing their subsequent action to this 'knowing', they will often justify their behaviour and decisions through the use of a logical argument.

As we have seen, intuition should definitely be developed as part of your set of leadership competencies. After all, the more you use your intuition, the more your intuition will serve you.

TRUST YOURSELF. YOU KNOW MORE THAN YOU THINK YOU DO.

Benjamin Spock

Final Thoughts

YOUR NEXT STEPS

THE IMPORTANCE OF LEADERSHIP DEVELOPMENT

In a report published by the international recruitment firm Randstad, in June 2013, it was highlighted that the top productivity challenge for 2014 is developing leadership skills to drive business growth, which coincides with the conclusions of "The State of Human Capital 2012" – a research study conducted by McKinsey & Company and The Conference Board.

The report emphasises that leadership development and succession management continue to be at the top of the current and future priorities for organisations, followed by talent acquisition and retention. However, it also underlines that only 35% of the human capital professionals are pursuing truly innovative approaches, with just 32% of those having high confidence in their strategy and actions.

The 4 key recommendations proposed by this report are:

- Anticipate and plan for the human capital of tomorrow.

- Secure a steady, reliable pipeline of skilled workers and tomorrow's leaders.

- Develop strategies to re-energise your employees' attitudes towards what they do and what the organisation stands for.

- Ensure that the human capital becomes more agile, as organisational agility is an essential response to the volatility of today's business environment.

Upon reviewing these recommendations, it is not hard to see that leadership continues to be at the centre of any successful enterprise; a trend that is unlikely to disappear in the near future.

So it is imperative for organisations that intend to operate successfully in the 21st century to foster an environment that enables continuous learning, teaches forward planning, and promotes agility, innovation and collaboration with others. This will be key to growing the individuals and leaders of the future; and to converting the work environment into a place where people can excel instead of merely survive.

Something to keep in mind is that organisations do not become innovative if their individual members are not given the opportunity to awaken their innovative spirit, nor do they become agile unless their staff learn how to be agile. Organisations can achieve high performance only if the brains of those who work for them make the right decisions, are able to influence others, deal with change effectively and function at an optimal level.

Allocating resources and time for individuals to adapt first has the power to transform any organisation. This requires measuring the existing state, using more current models and methodologies, changing processes to support the new learning, creating new habits and behaviours, re-measuring and reinforcing. The key is that these processes have to be applied to everyone from top to bottom – no exceptions.

As expressed in this book, the i4 Neuroleader Model proposes a novel approach of looking at leadership, and a more cost effective way to awaken the leadership powers within us, by first identifying our inner abilities and then learning how to use them more effectively. This model was developed to address the requirements of our new world and to make us realise that the constant distractions and the increasing pressure to do more with less does not make teams and organisations more effective or sustainable in the long term.

THE HUMAN RACE HAS ALWAYS BEEN
IN CONTINUOUS EVOLUTION AND NOW
IS NO DIFFERENT.

NEUROSCIENCE IS HELPING US
RECONSIDER THE VIEW WE HAVE OF
OURSELVES AND OUR WORK PRACTICES.

IT'S TIME FOR US TO UPDATE OUR
BEHAVIOURS AND BELIEFS.

HOW ABOUT YOU?
ARE YOU READY FOR THIS CHALLENGE?

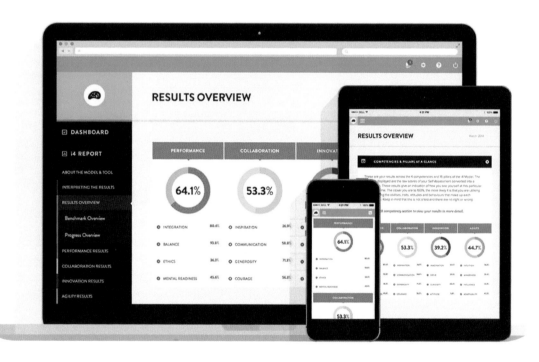

THE i4 NEUROLEADER ASSESSMENT TOOL

The i4 Neuroleader Model has been created as an easy-to-grasp framework for people who want to enhance their self-awareness and develop themselves, both as individuals and as leaders.

From this model and after years of research, our interdisciplinary team has designed a state-of-the-art assessment tool that embraces the latest neuroscience discoveries as they are applied to the field of leadership development and behavioural change.

With a simple click, any individual, consultant or organisation anywhere around the world can purchase and directly access this tool from any computer, tablet, iPad or mobile device.

FOR INDIVIDUALS

This assessment quantifies the areas of performance, collaboration, innovation and agility. Start your leadership journey by undertaking our Self or 360° Feedback questionnaire. Once you receive your i4 Neuroleader Report, you can chart your goals in the Reflection Workbook and have a life-changing conversation with one of our expert coaches.

FOR CONSULTANTS & COACHES

Consultants, coaches, psychologists, educators, HR practitioners and business leaders can become certified. This process makes you eligible to start utilising the i4 Neuroleader Assessments and Methodology with your clients, staff or students. The i4 Certification Programs are transformational in nature, helping you reconnect with your in-built human abilities.

FOR BUSINESS TEAMS

Any business, corporate, educational or volunteer group can take the initiative to assess themselves and their team's capabilities. Discover both the strengths and the limiting factors within your team.

For more information visit ⊕

www.aboutmybrain.com

REFERENCES & BIBLIOGRAPHY

Many books, journals, research papers and online resources have been consulted whilst writing this book.

With the purpose of making it easier for the reader, all the materials that have been reviewed are outlined below under the relevant chapter. No numbers associated with referencing have been used throughout the book.

CHAPTER 1

Books

1. Williams, L 2011, *Disrupt: Think the Unthinkable to Spark Transformation in Your Business*, Pearson Education, Inc.

Research Papers, Articles, Videos & Websites

2. Mansueto Ventures 2014, *Trusting Your Gut Makes all the Difference* <http://www.inc.com/dell/social-media-for-your-business.html?nav=pop>

3. Durkin, P & Gray, J 2013, *Crisis in Business Leadership*, Financial Review, <http://www.afr.com/p/boss/crisis_in_business_leadership_cq9NTG55IiPzqSLqvXbboM>

4. *Menlo Innovations* 2014, <http://www.menloinnovations.com>

5. The Ann Arbor News 2013, *Menlo Innovations continues to flourish with open and bossless office structure* <http://www.annarbor.com/business-review/menlo-innovations-continues-to-evangelize-open-and-bossless-office-structure/>

CHAPTER 2

Research Papers, Articles, Videos & Websites

1. Baer, R 2003, *Mindfulness Training as a Clinical Intervention: A Conceptual and Empirical Review*, Vol. 10, No.2, <http://www.wisebrain.org/papers/MindfulnessPsyTx.pdf>

2. Barker, B (Australian Human Resources Institute) 2013, *The Brain that changes itself,* HR Monthly Magazine, June Issue.

3. HR Daily 2012, *Our best picks of 2012: The Economy of the Neuroleader,* <http://www.hrdaily.com.au/nl06_news_selected.php?selkey=2459>

4. Langer, E & Moldoveanu, M 2000, *The Construct of Mindfulness*, Journal of Social Issues, Vol. 56, No.1, pp 1-9.

5. Ringleb, A & Rock, D 2009, *Neuroleadership in 2009*, Neuroleadership Journal, Issue 2, page 2.

6. Chapman, A adaption 2010, *Johari Window Model* (based on Ingham and Luft's original Johari Window Concept), Business Balls, <www.businessballs.com/johariwindowmodel>

7. Davidrock.net, *Bio: David Rock*, <www.davidrock.net/bio>

8. Ellington, L & McFadden, P 2012, *The Age of the NeuroLeader, The NeuroLeader Chronicles*, <http://www.neuroleader.us/2012/11/20/the-age-of-the-neuroleader/>

9. Von Tobel, A 2013, *Trusting Your Gut Makes All the DIfference*, Mansueto Ventures, <http://www.inc.com/dell/social-media-for-your-business.html?nav=pop>

CHAPTER 3

Books

1. Amen M.D., D 2009, *The Brain in Love: 12 Lessons to Enhance Your Love Life*, Harmony.

2. Amen M.D., D 2013, *Unleash the Power of the Female Brain*, Harmony.

3. Barsh, J, Cranston S & Lewis, G 2009, *How Remarkable Women Lead: The Breakthrough Model for Work and Life,* Crown Business.

4. Eliot Ph.D., L 2010, *Pink Brain, Blue Brain: How Small Differences Grow Into Troublesome Gaps -- And What We Can Do About It,* Mariner Books.

5. Feldhahn, S 2009, *The Male Factor: The Unwritten Rules, Mis-perceptions, and Secret Beliefs of Men in the Workplace*, Crown Business.

6. Hakim, C 2011, *Erotic Capital: The Power of Attraction in the Boardroom and the Bedroom*, Basic Books.

7. Helgesen, S, Johnson, J & Goldsmith, M 2010, *The Female Vision: Women's Real Power at Work*, Berrett-Koehler Publishers.

8. Moir, A & Jessel, D 1992, *Brain Sex: The Real Difference Between Men and Women*, Delta.

9. Roddick, A 1994, *Body and Soul: Profits with Principles -The Amazing Success Story of Anita Roddick & The Body Shop*, Three Rivers Press.

10. Sandberg, S 2013, *Lean in: Women, Work and the Will to Lead*, Borzoi Books

11. Tarr-Whelan, L 2011, *Women Lead the Way: Your Guide to Stepping Up to Leadership and Changing the World*, Berrett-Koehler Publishers.

12. Wong, A & Dawson, R 2010, *Secrets of Powerful Women: Leading Change for a New Generation,* Voice.

Research Papers, Articles, Videos & Websites

1. BizNetAU 2011, *In her shoes: Margaret Byrn (Part 1)*, YouTube, <http://www.youtube.com/watch?v=x7aTzHwLj8k>

2. Caumont, A 2013, *13 Data Milestones for 2013*, Pew Research Centre, <http://www.pewresearch.org/fact-tank/2013/12/23/13-data-milestones-for-2013/#utm_source=Dan+Pink%27s+Newsletter&utm_campaign=2392a21139-January_Newsletter1_1_2014&utm_medium=email&utm_term=0_4d8277f97a-2392a21139-306048865>

3. Daily Mail UK 2013, *'It will be easier for the next woman and I'm proud of that': Emotional farewell for tearful Julia Gillard as Kevin Rudd is sworn in a Australian PM*, <http://www.dailymail.co.uk/news/article-2349424/Julia-Gillards-emotional-farewell-Kevin-Rudd-sworn-Australian-PM-It-easier-woman.html>

4. Fisher PH.D., H 2013, *Gender DIfferences in the Brain*, USF College of Arts and Sciences [YouTube], <http://www.youtube.com/watch?v=qSGd6Ojuw0Q>

5. Genat, A, Wood, Prof. R & Victor, Dr. S 2012, *Gender Equality Project*, Centre for Ethical Leadership, Melbourne Business School.

6. Harvard Business Review 2013, *Vision Statement: Women & The Economics of Equality*, Harvard Business Publishing, <http://hbr.org/2013/04/women-and-the-economics-of-equality/ar/1>

7. Kovac, T 2013, F*irst Female PM a Job with No Guidelines,* Sydney Morning Herald Online, <http://www.smh.com.au/federal-politics/political-opinion/first-female-pm-a-job-with-no-guidelines-20130627-2oynl.html>

8. Pew Research Centre 2013, *10 Findings About Women in the Workplace,* <http://www.pewsocialtrends.org/2013/12/11/10-findings-about-women-in-the-workplace/>

9. Pew Research Centre 2013, *On Pay Gap, Millenial Women Near Parity – For Now,* <http://www.pewsocialtrends.org/2013/12/11/on-pay-gap-millennial-women-near-parity-for-now/>

10. Rosin, H 2010, *New Data on the Rise of Women*, TED talk, TED Conferences, LLC, <http://www.ted.com/talks/hanna_rosin_new_data_on_the_rise_of_women>

11. TEDx Talks 2013, *The most important lesson from 83,000 brain scans: Daniel Amen at TEDxOrangeCoast*, <http://www.youtube.com/watch?v=esPRsT-lmw8>

12. The Guardian 2013, *Male and female brains wired differently, scans reveal,* <http://www.theguardian.com/science/2013/dec/02/men-women-brains-wired-differently>

13. Williams, J 2013, M*eet the New Face of Diversity: The "Slacker" Millennial Guy*, Harvard Business Review Blog, <http://blogs.hbr.org/2013/10/meet-the-new-face-of-diversity-the-slacker-millennial-guy/>

14. The White House 2012, *Women Entrepreneurs are Creating Jobs: An Interactive Timeline*, <http://www.whitehouse.gov/women-entrepreneurs-jobs-timeline>

CHAPTER 4

Books

1. Fernandez, A 2013, *The ShapBrains Guide to Brain Fitness: How to Optimize Brain Health and Performance at Any Age*, SharpBrains Incorporated.

2. Godin, S 2012, *The Icarus Deception: How High Will You Fly?*, Portfolio Hardcover.

Research Papers, Articles, Videos & Websites

3. Co.Exist Staff 2013, *We Are Living in the Imagination Age--And We Can Shape Our Own Future*, Fast Company & Inc., <http://www.fastcoexist.com/1682472/we-are-living-in-the-imagination-age-and-we-can-shape-our-own-future>

4. Fernandez, A 2013, *10 Predicitions on How Digital Platforms Will Transform Brain Health in 2013*, Huffington Post, <http://www.huffingtonpost.com/alvaro-fernandez/brain-health_b_2479260.html>

5.   Kiefer, T 2011, *NeuroLeadership – Making Change Happen*, Ivey Business Journal, <http://www.iveybusinessjournal.com/topics/leadership/neuroleadership-–-making-change-happen#.UfNPuxYg0bk>

6.   *Neuroleadership Journal* 2009, Issue 2, <http://www.neuroleadership.org>

7.   Ringleb, Dr. Al H., Rock, Dr. D & Ancona, C 2012, *NeuroLeadership in 2011 & 2012*, NeuroLeadership Journal, Issue 4, <http://www.davidrock.net/files/01_NeuroLeadership_in_2011_and_2012_US.pdf>

8.   Williams, A 2013, *Great leaders are born, not made: Their brains are just wired differently, scientists say,* Daily Mail UK, <http://www.dailymail.co.uk/news/article-2307900/Natural-leaders-Study-claims-proof-commanding-figures-Churchill>

CHAPTER 5

Books

1.   Bass, B & Avolio, B 1993, *Improving Organisational Effectiveness through Transformational Leadership*, SAGE Publications.

2.   Bass, B & Riggio, R 2005, *Transformational Leadership*, Psychology Press.

3.   Bennis, W 1999, *Managing people is like herding cats*, Executive Excellence Publishing.

4.   Bennis, W & Thomas, R 2002, *Geeks and geezers*, Harvard Business Review Press.

5.   Bennis, W 2009, *On Becoming a Leader*, Basic books.

6.   Blanchard, K & Johnson, S 2003, *The one-minute manager*, William Morrow.

7.   Bohansen, B & Ryan, J 2012, *Leaders Make the Future: Ten New Leadership Skills for an Uncertain World*, Berrett-Koehler Publishers.

8.   Boyatzis, R & McKee, A 2005, *Resonant Leadership: Renewing yourself and connecting with others through Mindfulness, Hope and Compassion*, Harvard Business Review Press.

9.   Brizendine, L 2007, *The Female Brain,* Harmony.

10. Brizendine, L 2011, *The Male Brain*, Harmony.

11. Cubeiro, J & Gallardo, L 2010, *Mourinho versus Guardiola*, Alienta Editorial.

12. Dweck, C 2007, *Mindset: The New Psychology of Success*, Ballantine.

13. George, B 2004, *Authentic Leadership. Rediscovering the Secrets to Creating Lasting Value,* Jossey Bass.

14. Goleman, D 2005, *Emotional Intelligence. Why it Can Matter More than IQ*, 10th Anniversary Edition, Bantam Books.

15. Goleman, D 2000, *Working with Emotional Intelligence*, Bantam Books.

16. Goleman, D 2007, *Social Intelligence: The New Science of Social Relationships*, Bantam.

17. Goleman, D 2011, *The Brain and Emotional Intelligence: New Insights*, More than Sound.

18. Goleman, D 2013, *Focus: The Hidden Driver of Excellence*, Harper.

19. Goleman, D, Boyatzis, R & McKee, A 2013, *Primal Leadership: Unleashing the power of Emotional Intelligence*, 10th Anniversary Edition, Harvard Business Review Press.

20. Hennan, D & Bennis, W 1999, *Co-leaders: The power of great partnerships*, Wiley.

21. Hersey, P, Blanchard, K & Johnson, D 2012, *Management of Organizational Behaviour, Leading Human Resources*, 10th edition Prentice Hall.

22. Hersey, P 1985, *The Situational Leader*, Warner Books.

23. Kaplan, F 2008, *The Insurgents: David Petraeus and the plot to change the American way of war*, Simon Schuster.

24. Kotter, J 1988, *The Leadership Factor*, Free Press.

25. Kotter, J 2008, *A sense of urgency*, Harvard Business Press.

26. Kotter, J 2012, *Leading Change*, Harvard Business Press.

27. MacGregor Burns, J 2004, *Transforming Leadership*, Grove Press.

28. MacGregor Burns, J 2008, *Roosevelt. The soldier of freedom*, ACLS Humanities.

29. Mayer, J, Brackett, M & Salovey, P 2004, *Emotional Intelligence: Key Reading on the Mayer and Salovey Model*, National Professional Resources.

30. Nanus, B 1995, *Visionary Leadership*, Jossey Bass.

31. Prochaska, J, Norcross, J & DiClemente, C 2007, *Changing for good: A Revolutionary Six-Stage Program for Overcoming Bad Habits and Moving your Life Positively Forward*, William Morrow Paperbacks.

32. Taleb, N 2012, Nassim. *Antifragile: Things that gain from disorder*, Random House.

33. U. S. Army 2004, *Be, Know, Do: Leadership the Army way*, Jossey Bass.

34. Wren, J, Riggio, R & Genovese, M 2009, *Leadership and the Liberal Arts*, Jepson Studies in Leadership.

35. Zenger, J 2009, *The Extraordinary Leader: Turning Good Managers into Great Leaders,* McGraw-Hill.

36. Zenger, J 2009, *The Inspiring Leader: Unlocking the secrets of how the Extraordinary Leaders motivate,* McGraw-Hill.

CHAPTER 6

Books

1. Amen M.D., D 2011, *The Amen Solution: The Brain Healthy Way to Get Thinner, Smarter, Happier,* Harmony.

2. Amen M.D., D 2007, *The Brain in Love: 12 Lessons to Enhance Your Love Life*, Three Rivers Press.

3. Brown, S, Brown, R.M & Penner, L 2011, *Moving Beyond Self-Interest: Perspectives for Evolutionary Biology, Neuroscience, and the Social Sciences*, Oxford University Press, USA.

4. Dispenza, J 2012, *Breaking the Habit of Being Yourself: How to Lose Your Mind and Create a New One,* Hay House.

5. Ellerby PH.D., J 2010, *Inspiration Deficit Disorder: The No-Pill Prescription to End High Stress, Low Energy, and Bad Habits*, Hay House.

6. Gazzaniga,M & Le Doux, J 1978, *The Integrated Mind*, Plenum Press.

7. Goleman, D 1998, *Working With Emotional Intelligence*, Bantam Books.

8. Harung, Dr. H 1999, *Invincible Leadership: Building Peak Performance Organizations by Harnessing the Unlimited Power of Consciousness,* Maharishi University of Management. Joiner, W & Josephs, S 2006, Leadership Agility: Five Levels of Mastery for Anticipating and Initiating Change, Jossey-Bass.

9. Lieberman, M 2013, Social: Why Our Brains are Wired to Connect, Crown.

10. Schwartz, J & Gladding M.D., R 2011, *You Are Not Your Brain: The 4-Step Solution for Changing Bad Habits, Ending Unhealthy Thinking, and Taking Control of Your Life*, Avery.

11. Shinya, H 2012, *The Rejuvenation Enzyme: Reverse Ageing, Revitalize Cells, Restore Vigor,* Millichap Books.

12. Soosalu, G & Oka, M 2012, *mBraining: Using you Multiple Brains to do Cool Stuff*, CreateSpace Independent Publishing Platform, <www.mbraining.com>

Research Papers, Articles, Videos & Websites

13. Connolly, C, Ruderman, M & Lesli, JB 2013, *Sleep Well, Lead Well: How better sleep can improve leadership, boost productivity, and spark innovation*, Center for Creative Leadership. Lieberman, M 2013, Should Leaders Focus on Results, or on People?, Harvard Business Review Blog Network, <http://blogs.hbr.org/2013/12/should-leaders-focus-on-results-or-on-people/>

14. Salovey, P & Mayer, J.D. 1989-90, *Imagination, Cognition, and Personality,* Vol. 9, No. 3, pp185-211.

15. Yuhas, D 2013, *Kind Hearts are Healthier*, Scientific American, <http://www.scientificamerican.com/article/kind-hearts-are-healthier/>

CHAPTER 7

Books

1. Brown, J & Fenske, M 2010, *The Winner's Brain: 8 Strategies Great Minds Use to Achieve Success*, First Da Capo Press Edition.

2. Dispenza, J 2007, *Evolve Your Brain: The Science of Changing Your Mind*, HCI.

3. Harung Ph.D., H & Travis, F 2012, *Higher mind-brain development in successful leaders testing unified theory of performance*, Springer, <http://link.springer.com/article/10.1007/s10339-011-0432-x> Lipton, B 2008, The Biology of Belief: Unleashing the Power of Consciousness, Matter, & Miracles, Hay House.

4. McGonigal, K 2012, *The Willpower Instinct: How Self-Control Works, Why It Matters, and What You Can Do To Get More of It*, Penguin Group.

5. Pert Ph.D., C 1999, *Molecules of Emotion: The Science Behind Mind-Body Medicine*, Simon & Schuster.

6. Pert Ph.D., C & Marriot, N 2007, *Everything You Need to Know to Feel Go(o)d*, Hay House.

7. Robbins, J 2008, *A Symphony in the Brain: The Evolution of the New Brain Wave Biofeedback*, Grove Press.

8. Siegel, D 2012, *The Developing Mind, Second Edition: How Relationships and the Brain Interact to Shape Who We Are,* The Guilford Press, 2nd Edition.

9. Siegel, D 2010, *Mindsight: The New Science of Personal Transformation*, Bantam.

Research Papers, Articles, Videos & Websites

1. Cooper, R 2000, *A new neuroscience of leadership: bringing out more of the best in people, Strategy & Leadership*, Vol. 28, Issue 6, pp. 11-15

2. Department of Psychiatry, Washington University St Louis, *Depression Facts*, <http://www.psychiatry.wustl.edu/depression/depression_facts.htm>

3. e! Science News 2009, *Transcendental Meditation buffers students against college stress: Study, Psychology & Sociology,* <http://esciencenews.com/articles/2009/02/24/transcendental.meditation.buffers.students.against.college.stress.study>

4. Editors, The 2003, *Get Real*, Scientific American Magazine, <http://www.scientificamerican.com/article/get-real/>

5. Fox, E 2013, *Tune Your Subliminal Biases toward Optimism*, Scientific American Magazine - Mind, <http://www.scientificamerican.com/article/tune-your-subliminal-biases-toward-optimism/>

6. Harung, H, Travis, F, Blank,W & Heaton, D 2009, *Higher development, brain integration, and excellence in leadership*, Emerald Group Publishing Limited

7. Markowitz, E 2013, *Inside the Brain of a Leader*, <http://www.inc.com/magazine/201306/eric-markowitz/brain-leadership-inside.html>

8. Orsatti, M 2011, *New research looks at brain integration in top athletes and in long-time meditators*, Transcendental Meditation Blog <https://www.tm.org/blog/research/brain-integration-in-top-athletes/>

9. PBS Online 2011, *Crash of Flight 447*, <http://www.pbs.org/wgbh/nova/space/crash-flight-447.html>

10. Siegel, D 2009, *On Integrating the Two Hemispheres of Our Brains*, < https://www.youtube.com/watch?v=xPjhfUVgvOQ>

11. Stix, G 2013, *The Neuroscience of True Grit*, Scientific American Magazine - Mind, <http://www.scientificamerican.com/article/the-neuroscience-of-true-grit/>

12. The University of Queensland 2010, *The Integrated Brain (NEUR3002)*, <http://www.uq.edu.au/study/course.html?course_code=NEUR3002&offer=53544c554332494e&year=2010>

13. Strayer, D & Watson, J 2012, *Top Multitaskers Help Explain How Brain Juggles Thoughts*, Scientific American Magazine - Mind, <http://www.scientificamerican.com/article/supertaskers-and-the-multitasking-brain/>

14. Wikipedia 2014, *Air France Flight 447*, <www.wikipedia.org/wiki/Air_France_Flight_447>

CHAPTER 8

Research Papers, Articles, Videos & Websites

1. Merriam-Webster 2014, *Enthusiasm*, <http://www.merriam-webster.com/dictionary/enthusiasm>

2. Merriam-Webster 2014, *Inspirative*, <http://www.merriam-webster.com/dictionary/inspirative>

CHAPTER 9

Books

1. De Bono, E 1985, *Six Thinking Hats*, Penguin Books.

2. Kirkwood, K 2012, *The Power of Imagination*, Destiny Image.

3. Lehrer, J 2012, *Imagine: How Creativity Works*, Houghton Mifflin.

Research Papers, Articles, Videos & Websites

1. ABC1 Australia 2013, *Redesign my Brain*, Series 1, Mindful Media, <http://mindfulmedia.com.au/redesign-my-brain>

2. Gregoire, C 2013, *Research Uncovers How And Where Imagination Occurs In The Brain*, Hufftington Post, <http://www.huffingtonpost.com/2013/09/17/imagination-brain_n_3922136.html>

3. Moulton, S & Kosslyn, S 2009, *Imagining predictions: mental imagery as mental emulation*, Royal Society Publishing.

CHAPTER 10

Books

1.	Day, L 1997, *Practical Intuition*, Broadway Books.

2.	Jung, C.G. 1912, *Pschologische Typen*, Zurich: Rasher. [Translated by Hull, RF.C.,1971, Psychological Types. Collected Works, Vol 10. London: Routledge & Kegan Paul]. Mierczarech, V 2009, Inteligencia Intuitiva, Editorial Kairos.

3.	Nataraja, Dr. S 2008, *The Blissful Brain: Neuroscience and Proof of the Power of Meditation (Gaia Thinking)*, Gaia Book Ltd.

Research Papers, Articles, Videos & Websites

1.	Gigerenzer, G 2011, *The Role of Intuitions*, Go Cognitive, <http://www.gocognitive.net/interviews/role-intuitions>

2.	Patton, JR 2003, *Intuition in Decisions*, Emerald Insights, <http://www.emeraldinsight.com/journals.htm?articleid=865460&show=abstract>

3.	Sadler-Smith, E 2013, *Professor of Organisational Behaviour*, University of Surrey, <http://www.surrey.ac.uk/sbs/people/eugene_sadlersmith/>

4.	Young, E 2012, *Gut Instincts: The secrets of your second brain*, New Scientist Magazine, December Issue, < http://www.newscientist.com/article/mg21628951.900-gut-instincts-the-secrets-of-your-second-brain.html>

i4 NEUROLEADER WORKBOOK →

AVAILABLE ON AMAZON

www.leadershipupsidedown.com

THE POETRY OF LEADERSHIP →

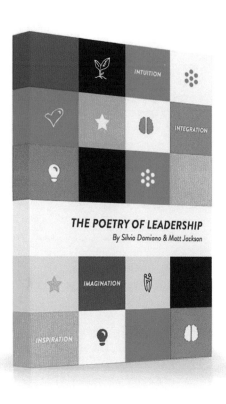

THE POETRY OF LEADERSHIP
By Silvia Damiano & Matt Jackson

AVAILABLE ON AMAZON

www.leadershipupsidedown.com

OTHER BOOKS BY SILVIA DAMIANO →

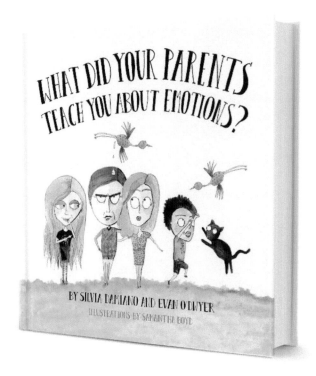

LEADERSHIP IS UPSIDE DOWN
THE i4 NEUROLEADER REVOLUTION

A book by Silvia Damiano
in collaboration with Juan Carlos Cubeiro & Tao de Haas

Published by
About my Brain™
About my Brain Institute Pty. Ltd.
PO Box 163
Neutral Bay Junction
NSW 2089 Australia

Email   hello@aboutmybrain.com
Web   www.aboutmybrain.com

First published in May 2014
This edition was edited in August 2015
ISBN978-0-9924803-3-2

Cover, design, illustrations by Relmi Damiano
Editing & Proofreading by Morweena Shahani, Melissa Dumas, Pandora Varley, Elleanor Kearsley

6 5 4 3 2

LEGAL CONSIDERATIONS

Made in the USA
Charleston, SC
20 October 2016